STARTING YOUR OWN BUSINESS

AN ENTREPRENEUR'S GUIDE TO
STARTING AND GROWING A SMALL
BUSINESS

Nevin M. Buconjic, MBA

Digital Adventures
Sault Ste. Marie, Ontario

Second Edition – Revised and Updated, August 2018.

Copyright © 2012, 2018 Nevin M. Buconjic. All rights reserved, including the right to reproduce this book, or portions thereof, in any form. No part of this text may be reproduced, transmitted, downloaded, decompiled, reverse engineered, or stored in or introduced into any information storage and retrieval system, in any form or by any means, whether electronic or mechanical without the express written permission of the author. The scanning, uploading, and distribution of this book via the Internet or via any other means without the permission of the publisher is illegal and punishable by law. The publisher does not have any control over and does not assume any responsibility for author or third-party websites or their content.

Limit of liability/Disclaimer of Warranty: While the publisher and author have used their best efforts in preparing this book, they make no representations or warranties with respect to the accuracy or completeness of the contents in this book and specifically disclaim any implied warranties or merchantability of fitness for a particular purpose. The advice and strategies contained herein may not be suitable for your situation. Neither the publisher nor author shall be liable for any loss or profit or other commercial damages, including but not limited to special, incidental, consequential or other damages.

Published by: Digital Adventures
www.digitaladventures.ca

Starting Your Own Business: An Entrepreneur's Guide to Starting and Growing a Business

Nevin M. Buconjic – Second Edition
ISBN-13:978-1724549709

This book is dedicated to my parents for always believing in me, and to my wife Kristy, who supported me throughout this project -- including editing multiple versions. I couldn't have done it without you.

I also want to thank Bob Minhas, Founder at Entrepreneur House for sharing his insights on business planning and the Business Model Canvas in this book.

TABLE OF CONTENTS

PREFACE 1

INTRODUCTION 5

CHAPTER 1 - AM I AN ENTREPRENEUR? 7

CHAPTER 2 - THE BIG IDEA 13

CHAPTER 3 - MARKET RESEARCH 45

CHAPTER 4 - THE BUSINESS PLAN 55

CHAPTER 5 – BUSINESS PLAN ALTERNATIVES 71

CHAPTER 6 - FUNDING YOUR BUSINESS......................... 85

CHAPTER 7 – PREPARING TO LAUNCH............................. 91

CHAPTER 8 - GETTING YOUR BUSINESS ONLINE 101

CHAPTER 9 – THE LAUNCH 107

CHAPTER 10 - PROMOTING YOUR BUSINESS 113

CHAPTER 11 - LEVERAGING SOCIAL MEDIA 125

CHAPTER 12 - I'M IN BUSINESS, NOW WHAT? 137

CHAPTER 13 – SIDE HUSTLE CASE STUDY 141

RECOMMENDED RESOURCES 147

ABOUT THE AUTHOR 150

ENDNOTES 151

PREFACE

I have had an entrepreneurial drive for as long as I can remember. I was taught the importance of earning my own money at an early age; and this inspired me to think of some creative ways to make money as a child and indirectly put me on the path of entrepreneurship. At the age of 10, I had my own newspaper route, and by age 12, I was selling home and novelty gifts from Regal Greetings & Gifts catalogues to my neighbors.

Later, I majored in business at university, and participated in Students in Free Enterprise (now Enactus). My first "real" business was selling personal computers and software out of my bedroom.

After completing my MBA, I worked for several years in the finance and banking sectors -- but I just wasn't fulfilled. I decided to merge my world of business and passion for technology — I quit my job, moved back home and completed a third "accelerated" degree in computer science over 12 months.

I went on to co-found a web design company and create Adventures in Computing summer camps before I started my consulting business, Digital Adventures. The computer camps business operated seasonally for 10 years, and we taught over a thousand kids aged 7-15 about web development, computing and game design (2D and 3D), before I sold the business. Over that time, I learned a tremendous amount about building a business, customer service, curriculum development, staffing, and marketing on a budget.

Early in the growth of my business, I accepted a job opportunity to help young entrepreneurs start and grow businesses, through our local economic development agency. I was tasked with running numerous government programs including loans, grants, and awareness programs. I spoke to thousands of students about being an entrepreneur and starting their own business. I helped hundreds of entrepreneurs start and grow their businesses over a four-year period, as I advanced through the ranks to Business Advisor and Manager.

It was a turning point in my career, because I realized how much I enjoyed helping entrepreneurs and speaking to students about entrepreneurship. I eventually left to work for government in a business analyst/advisor role, but never let go of my entrepreneurial dreams and passion.

In the nearly 15 years since, I have started four new businesses while working full-time in government and economic development. I have embraced the idea of side hustles, or side gigs as they are referred to in the new economy. For many years, as my career was pulled deeper into the depths and bureaucracy of government, my only relief was the excitement of spending time building my businesses in the evenings.

A few years ago, I left government to return to an economic development role, and I continue to operate a relatively new business – BrandMe.social, a resume development and personal branding consultancy part-time, because I love being an entrepreneur.

Today there are so many opportunities to make money with your skills and talents, through freelancing and starting a side gig separate from your day job. Seven of the eight businesses I have started were part-time businesses. They were low risk and didn't require significant startup funds. I am such a fan of side hustles that I wrote my first book, *25 Money-Making Businesses You Can Start in Your Spare Time,* drawing on my experiences and those of my clients.

In 2013 I founded StartUP Sault Ste. Marie, a volunteer organization (part of the Startup Canada network) to build a startup community in Sault Ste. Marie to connect local entrepreneurs and innovators with available business resources, and to each other. We connect our members through regular meetups such as Startup Drinks, Startup Book Club and Startup Boot Camps. Startup Talks features successful local entrepreneurs telling their stories, and Startup Pitch Nights helps promote local startups, while they compete for cash prizes. We also hold monthly mentorship meetings to support each other through our entrepreneurial journeys.

Being an entrepreneur isn't always easy and can sometimes be lonely – especially if you work out of your basement. Joining a network of entrepreneurs in your community can help provide the support and comradery that you need to succeed.

In 2017 I was awarded the Startup Canada Entrepreneur Promotion Award for advancing the environment and culture of entrepreneurship in Canada. It was a rewarding moment.

Over the course of my career I have mentored, taught and spoken to thousands of entrepreneurs, teens and adults about business, technology and entrepreneurship. I am passionate about these topics, and about empowering people to explore entrepreneurship. I hope this book will do just that for you.

Nevin M. Buconjic, B.Sc., MBA, BA

INTRODUCTION

I contemplated writing this book for many years. As an entrepreneur myself, I have learned many valuable lessons over the years. Working with budding entrepreneurs to start and grow their own businesses has been a very rewarding experience.

Starting Your Own Business: An Entrepreneur's Guide to Starting and Growing a Small Business is written for new entrepreneurs exploring the idea of starting their own business, with a slant toward launching a business on a budget. Every one of my businesses have been bootstrapped, or grown through low-cost techniques and strategies, without significant investment and risk. Whether you are just graduating from college, feel stuck in a job you don't enjoy, or you are looking to capitalize on a new opportunity, you can start your own business using the tools found in this book.

In the following chapters, you will learn what makes entrepreneurs successful, how to discover and validate a great idea for your business, and the steps involved in planning and launching your business. You will learn how to perform market research, write a business plan, obtain funding, promote your business, and access the help you need along the way (usually for free).

Throughout this book I will provide examples from my own experience, as well as others I have worked with, and will refer to specific resources or programs available in Canada and the United States. To help even further, we include web links throughout the book and at the end of each chapter. In the ebook version of this book, the links are clickable.

For the paperback version, you can easily access all the links by visiting our resource page at:

www.nevinbuconjic.com/resources.html

The number of resources, funding opportunities and support available today for entrepreneurs today is amazing. You are not alone in this journey.

I truly believe that starting your own business can be one of the best decisions of your life, and the support exists more than ever to make it a reality.

CHAPTER 1 - AM I AN ENTREPRENEUR?

Entrepreneurs are special individuals. They possess common traits and skills which allow them to be successful in business and in life.

Some argue that entrepreneurs are born not made...that they possess these skills and are destined for greatness. Others argue that while entrepreneurs are born with certain characteristics, their upbringing, education and experience are equally responsible for their success. What do you think?

What can be agreed upon is that not everyone is an entrepreneur, and those who are, possess a number of common traits such as those listed below:

20 Common Traits of Entrepreneurs

- Goal oriented
- Confidence
- Competitive
- Self-starter
- Persistence
- Passionate
- Recognizes opportunities
- Resourcefulness
- Strong work ethic
- Ability to adapt to change
- Disciplined
- Courage
- Ability to handle stress
- Independent
- Creativity
- Strong people skills
- Ability to accept risk
- Open minded
- Vision
- Ability to see the big picture

Successful entrepreneurs possess most if not all of the traits above. Do you see traits above that you have as well?

If you aren't sure whether you are an entrepreneur, or just aren't convinced, there are several online tests and assessments available that can help you decide.

The Entrepreneur Next Door - Entrepreneurship Test
http://theentrepreneurnextdoor.com/tests/entrepreneurship.html

The Only Entrepreneur Test You Will Ever Need - Forbes.com
www.forbes.com/sites/aileron/2012/06/04/the-only-entrepreneur-test-you-will-ever-need/

Business Development Bank of Canada - Entrepreneurial Potential Self-assessment
www.bdc.ca/en/articles-tools/entrepreneur-toolkit/business-assessments/pages/self-assessment-test-your-entrepreneurial-potential.aspx

Examples of Successful Entrepreneurs

There are many examples of successful entrepreneurs who have changed the way we do things.

Classic Entrepreneurs

Classic entrepreneurs might include Henry Ford, who invented the assembly line for the production of automobiles. This allowed for the rapid production of affordable automobiles which changed the way people travelled and led to the development of highway systems and efficient transportation across nearly every continent.

Thomas Edison, while certainly one of the greatest inventors of all time, also commercialized many of his inventions including the light bulb, phonograph and motion-picture camera.

> **"I have not failed. I've just found 10,000 ways that won't work."** – *Thomas Edison*

Another example is Ray Kroc, who took McDonald's from a single restaurant to one of the most successful franchises and well-known brands in the world. Ray did not start McDonald's, but he purchased it from the founders and created the McDonald's we all know today -- because he believed the concept could be very successful on a larger scale.

> *"I didn't invent the hamburger. I just took it more seriously than anyone else...We take the hamburger business more seriously than anyone else."-- Ray Kroc*

Ok, so you might need to open the history books to read about those entrepreneurs, but how about a few more modern examples?

Steve Jobs

Steve Jobs, the brilliant visionary and co-founder of Apple Inc. (formerly Apple Computer). Steve Jobs had his share of successes and failures and was even fired from Apple in 1985.

He started or purchased a stake in several other businesses (including Pixar, the animation studio that brought us Toy Story and Finding Nemo), before returning to Apple in 1997 as it teetered on the brink of failure. He managed to turn the company around by slashing their product line and focusing on creating revolutionary products, that were different than anything else on the market. Jobs also had a gift for knowing what consumers wanted, sometimes even before they knew themselves.

"You can't ask customers what they want and then try to give that to them. By the time you get it built, they'll want something new." – *Steve Jobs*

Some of the products he led the creation of included the iMac, iPod, iTunes (digital ecosystem for music, books, videos), iPhone and iPad. Not to mention the original Macintosh computer which changed the way we interact with computers -- by using a mouse and graphical user interface.

Shortly before his death in October 2011 from Pancreatic Cancer, Apple surpassed Exxon Mobile Corp. as the most valuable company in the world -- something that might have seemed impossible just a decade earlier. Even more incredible, on August 2, 2018, Apple became the first publicly traded company in the world to hit a $1 trillion market cap!

Richard Branson

Richard Branson started his first business at the age of 16 and created Virgin Records, a mail order record company, a few years later.[1] He went on to launch Virgin Airways, Virgin Mobile and numerous other businesses. Today his company, the Virgin Group, operates more than 400 companies, including Virgin Galactic a space tourism company!

"Business opportunities are like buses, there's always another one coming." – *Richard Branson*

Branson is another example of a risk-taking visionary who seized upon both ideas and opportunities and is now one of the richest people in the world.

Mark Zuckerberg

Mark Zuckerberg is perhaps one of the most famous Internet entrepreneurs of all time. The creator of Facebook, the world's largest social network, Zuckerberg started the website in 2004 with several friends, while a sophomore at Harvard University.

Originally designed for college and university students, the social network exploded in popularity and has since grown to over two billion users. Zuckerberg has become very successful and very wealthy along the way. Facebook went public in May 2012 with a valuation of $100 billion, making Zuckerberg and many other employees and investors billionaires. By 2018 the company was worth over $600 billion.

"Serving more people, increasing your customer base and making them more deeply engaged is by itself good business." [2] *- Mark Zuckerberg*

There are many more examples of extraordinarily successful entrepreneurs. But success doesn't have to mean creating an Internet company that goes public and makes you a millionaire. Success is dictated not only by financial gain, but the knowledge and experiences acquired along the way.

There are millions of entrepreneurs around the world achieving daily success on their own terms, running their own part-time, full-time or even seasonal businesses.

While today's ultra-successful entrepreneurs are often likened to rock stars, and sometimes make their accomplishments seem easy, this couldn't be further from the truth.

Successful entrepreneurs have often sacrificed and struggled to make their businesses a success. Luck and timing can play a huge part in success as well. They may make it look easy, but don't expect things to always run smoothly.

But if you are like me, the thought of building a business and making money doing something you truly enjoy, challenges included, creates a sense of accomplishment that is difficult to achieve elsewhere.

CHAPTER 2 - THE BIG IDEA

You picked up this book to learn how to start a business, and chances are you may already have an idea for a business you'd like to start. Even if you think your idea is great, unique, or a huge opportunity, it is important to ground the idea by doing some research to validate the market opportunities and identify potential challenges.

We will learn more about market research in the next chapter, but one of the biggest challenges for new entrepreneurs or wannabe entrepreneurs is coming up with the right idea.

"All achievements, all earned riches, have their beginning in an idea." *– Napoleon Hill*

Many people dream of starting their own business but haven't found an opportunity or figured out what kind of business to start. One of the first steps for developing a business idea is to think in terms of what skills, talents or experience you already possess, and what opportunities this might create. You may have taught yourself how to build websites, and found that you were really good at it, or you may have worked in an industry for many years and figured out a better way of doing things. These could be opportunities to monetize your skills by starting your own business.

Most businesses are created to capitalize on perceived opportunities to satisfy the needs of society or specific markets. If you can provide a solution to a problem, using skills that people value, in a niche you are passionate about, then you have the chance to make money doing what you enjoy[3]. An elusive dream for many.

If you are serious about starting your own business, but aren't sure what kind of business to start, then I suggest you begin by doing the following exercise:

Make a list of all your skills, experience (accomplishments), hobbies and talents. Now look at your list. Are there any patterns, specialized skills or knowledge? What kind of business could you start that would benefit from and utilize these skills and experience for profit? Write down everything that comes to mind. Don't worry if some may seem unrealistic.

Perhaps you collect comic books, or toy figurines. One idea could be to buy and sell comic books or figurines on eBay or other online marketplaces such as Amazon.com. Perhaps you could start a blog sharing your knowledge, and insights on the topic with the collectibles community. If you could build a large enough audience, further opportunities such as paid advertising or sponsored posts could materialize. These are just simple ideas based on something you are already passionate about. Imagine the possibilities!

Next, think of any products or services that you like, use or enjoy but aren't available in your area. What did you come up with? Could your own business provide these products or services? Do you think there are enough people who would pay for these products or services? If so, you could have a business opportunity on your hands. Of course, you will have to flesh out your idea by doing some market research which you will learn about in the next chapter.

"I never perfected an invention that I did not think about in terms of the service it might give others… I find out what the world needs, then I proceed to invent." – Thomas Edison

Another method for finding business ideas is to see what trends and developments are on the horizon. Pick up a copy business magazines such as Entrepreneur and Fast Company or visit www.trendhunter.com and www.entrepreneur.com for ideas. These sources typically highlight new, cutting-edge businesses and emerging ideas and trends.

Depending on your areas of interest, you should follow developments in particular industries or key companies in the sector. Staying on top of new products, services and other developments in the industry could spark some ideas for your own business -- particularly smaller niches or spinoff ideas.

You can even setup Google Alerts to send you an email every time your keywords pop up in the news or on the web. Google will notify you automatically.

Read everything you can get your hands on about your area of interest. This could be books, magazines, company annual reports etc. The more you stay on top of the sector or industry, the better chance you will have of identifying new opportunities.

What if you still don't have any ideas for the kind of business you can start?

I may be able to help. In my book, 25 Money-Making Businesses You Can Start in Your Spare Time, I have researched and identified 25 businesses that almost anyone can start, with reasonable startup costs. Although some of the ideas require specialized skills, many of the business ideas are from my own experiences working with entrepreneurs, including web design, photography, lawn care and cupcake businesses. They have done it and you can too!

Below are ten examples of businesses you can start part-time or full-time. I recommend starting part-time and growing your business over time. This lowers the risk dramatically. Reinvest your earnings and try different things. Don't be afraid to fail.

Affiliate Marketing

Affiliate marketing has been around for years. Affiliate marketing on the Internet was made popular by Amazon.com and other online retailers who pay a commission every time an affiliate sends traffic to their site, and a purchase is made.

There are still good affiliate programs available online, and one strategy has always been to create a website or blog focused on a particular niche area, create content on the topic to drive search engine traffic to the site, and then plaster the site with affiliate ads.

Online advertising has evolved since then to include programs like Google Adsense which displays appropriate ads on your website based on the content, and then you are paid by Google for the number of clicks each ad receives (pay-per-click or PPC).

Through a combination of affiliate marketing and PPC type programs, it is still possible to bring in revenue from your website. But the secret is to promote relevant products and services to your own loyal following. Your email list is much more powerful at converting sales, than visitors to your website.

It is important to build your email list by asking readers and customers to sign up to receive information from you. The growth of social media has also created another opportunity for affiliate marketers, but it is not nearly as effective as email marketing.

Typically there are several factors necessary to make significant revenue through affiliate programs. These include large volumes of traffic to your website or blog, a growing email list, and a lot of social media followers. It can be easier to grow a large following on Twitter or Facebook than subscribers to your blog, but most Internet marketers still believe email marketing is more lucrative.

Promoting affiliate products to these channels can be effective, provided the products are relevant to your niche, high quality and the sales copy is convincing.

It is important to remember that you have built a trusting relationship with your readers and followers -- therefore offers should only be sent out for products you truly do believe in. Your readers will appreciate that you are sending them useful information and tools to help them.

There are a number of excellent affiliate networks and programs on the Internet. According to The Online Advertising Blue Book, the top five affiliate (CPS) networks in 2018 are:

Rakuten Affiliate Network (www.rakutenmarketing.com/)
Awin Group/ShareASale (www.shareasale.com)
CJ Affiliate by Conversant (www.cj.com)
eBay Partner Network (https://partnernetwork.ebay.com/)
Amazon (https://affiliate-program.amazon.com/)

I suggest you check out each of them to see if they are a good fit for you. Each affiliate network has multiple programs within it, from different retailers -- including top names like Walmart, Amazon, AT&T, and Barnes & Noble.

I have personally purchased information products and WordPress plugins via ShareASale and JVZoo.com and have been very pleased. In fact, I was so impressed by the products I have used as a consumer/business owner, that I became an affiliate for these sites myself.

Affiliate marketing is alive and well and can create a significant stream of income for you if you have the ability to reach targeted audiences via your websites, blogs, email lists and social media.

For more information, explore the following links:

What is Affiliate Marketing? A Guide for Beginners
https://moreniche.com/blog/beginners-guide-affiliate-marketing/

How to Start an Online Affiliate Business
www.seodesignsolutions.com/blog/how-to-reference-material/how-to-start-an-online-affiliate-business

The Definitive Guide to Affiliate Marketing
www.forbes.com/sites/robertadams/2017/05/25/the-definitive-guide-to-affiliate-marketing/#56e2ac0675ff

How to Start a Profitable Online Business with Affiliate Marketing
www.thebalancesmb.com/affiliate-marketing-4161605

Online Retailer

Online sales continue to grow each year. Popular online retailers like Amazon.com and Overstock.com have billions of dollars in sales annually. Every major brand and retailer has an online presence and the majority sell directly online as well. How can you compete with these giants?

The secret to starting your own successful online retail business is to focus on a niche market. Perhaps you make your own products such as woodworking, crafts or other unique items. Maybe you collect comic books, Star Wars figurines or trading cards. You can sell these products online on your own website, eBay or other e-commerce platforms like Amazon, Facebook or [Shopify](), a very popular ecommerce platform.

If you are reselling products, you will want to ensure that you have reliable suppliers, and enough space to store inventory. It is next to impossible to compete with larger, established e-commerce sites for many reasons. The secret is to build a community around selling products that very few others are selling.

The name of your online store will be important. It should be easy to remember and typically should reflect what you are selling, or some characteristic of your business. But there are also plenty of examples of online stores with curious names like Zappos.com, Amazon.com or even Etsy.com.

Choose carefully and purchase the domain name right away. In most cases the .com extension is the universally accepted and most appealing domain name extension. But there are newer options like .shop, .trade, .shopping and .store that offer up alternatives to the norm. Choosing a domain with a country extension such as .ca for Canada is also acceptable in many cases but be careful not to limit your market from the get-go.

When developing your marketing and advertising strategies, focus on your target market. How can you best reach these buyers?

This might involve advertising on Facebook, specialized or local websites, doing a combination of print and web marketing, or using traditional channels like TV and radio. It will depend on your business.

Whatever the method, the idea is to drive traffic to your site and convert this traffic into sales.

Other considerations are physical space requirements (do you need to hold inventory?), staffing (can you run this business yourself?), customer service, etc.

As with any new business, you should do your research and check out the competition.

Drafting a business plan could help flesh out your idea even more and forecast the kinds of costs involved in such a project.

As mentioned earlier, you may wish to start by utilizing eBay and other low-cost platforms or webstores before spending any money developing your own e-commerce website. Think of it as a test to see if there truly is a market for your products.

Visit these websites for more information, tips and ideas:

Shopify Business Name Generator
www.shopify.co.uk/tools/business-name-generator

20 Killer Tips to Create a Successful Online Store
www.sellbrite.com/blog/20-killer-tips-to-create-a-successful-online-store/

Selling Online with Fulfillment by Amazon

Did you know that you can sell products on Amazon.com and have Amazon collect the payment, ship the order and even stock all of your inventory?

Amazon's Fulfillment-by-Amazon (FBA) program has changed the game for online sellers and created one of the greatest opportunities for people like you and me to build successful online businesses in no time at all.

Thousands of individuals are utilizing this platform to sell millions of products every day on Amazon.com.

One of the benefits of selling on Amazon is the credibility and trust that already exists with its customers. Amazon typically offers the best prices, and exceptional customer service (including return policies) – which makes selling on Amazon so easy.

For a monthly fee (currently $40) you can sign up for a professional seller account through Amazon's Seller Central and start your business today. Simply create your product listing(s), ship your inventory to Amazon's own warehouses, and start selling. Amazon also takes a percentage of your sales as fees for using the program and can charge storage fees based on your inventory.

There are numerous books and courses you can take to learn more about this business opportunity. I personally enrolled in a course myself and in July 2014 I started my business selling my own brand of products (including electronics, and houseware products) on Amazon. I was amazed at how easy the concept was and how much potential there truly is to make money using this business model.

Although almost everything I learned in the course could have been learned through trial and error, going through a complete training program allowed me to get up and running within a short period of time. Regardless of the training program, the key concepts are quite similar.

I will summarize them below:

1. Find a Product(s) – There are various techniques for finding potentially successful products to sell, but the bottom line is you want to find products that are in high demand (competitive categories), are relatively small and light weight (to keep Amazon storage fees and shipping costs low), and typically retail for between $7-40 dollars (to keep inventory costs low).

2. Source Your Product(s) – Find reliable wholesalers, distributors or manufacturers that will supply your products to you at prices that allow for a healthy profit margin. You may wish to consider utilizing www.alibaba.com to source low-cost products from China.

3. Create Your Own Brand(s) and private label your products. This technique allows you to differentiate your products from other companies and brands.

4. Create killer Amazon Listings – This step alone can help distinguish your brand from the competition. Many companies (even leading brands) sell their products on Amazon as just another sales outlet and do little to make their product listings compelling – instead just relying on their brand name. By focusing on optimizing your title, description and product images you can have your product listing stand out from the competition!

5. Marketing and Promotion – It will be up to you to market and promote your Amazon products utilizing social media, press releases, getting blogger reviews, and even paid advertising on Facebook, Google Ads or other methods. Strong marketing efforts can drive significant traffic to your sales pages on Amazon.

6. Reviews are King – Another way that Amazon customers benefit is through product reviews. Most customers considering buying something from Amazon will read the reviews to see if the product is good quality and meets the expectations of existing customers. This can create a huge advantage for sellers that focus on getting reviews from their customers. Amazon allows you to follow up with customers and provide effective customer service. This can include asking for product reviews, and let's face it, the more positive reviews your product has, the easier it will be to make the sale.

7. Customer Service – Most programs teach you to focus on providing excellent customer service in order to stand apart from the competition. This may include following up on customer emails/inquiries, offering free replacement items and responding to any negative reviews quickly. Simply going out of your way to provide an excellent buying experience will help create loyal repeat customers, build your brand and increase your sales in the long run.

There are many other techniques that can be learned to build a successful Amazon business, but at the end of the day you want to build a successful brand, offer quality products and deliver exceptional customer service.

The level of success you can reach with an Amazon business is almost limitless with the right products, branding and ratings.

Many Amazon entrepreneurs start small and re-invest profits in their business – allowing them to invest more in product inventory (including customization and branding) and promotion.

While I have just scratched the surface of building a successful business on Amazon, I encourage you to learn more about this opportunity and see what is possible for yourself.

Below is a list of resources for further information:

Amazon Services - FBA
http://services.amazon.com/content/fulfillment-by-amazon.htm

Guide to Starting a Fulfillment by Amazon Business
www.entrepreneur.com/article/282277

The Proven Amazon Course (PAC)
www.provenamazoncourse.com/

Amazing Selling Machine
www.amazingsellingmachine.com

Digital Info Product Author (ebooks)

The Internet and proliferation of digital devices has changed the way people access information, and even read books and magazines. Digital versions of print books are often less expensive and more convenient to access and purchase.

While it took many years to fully catch on, with the success of the Amazon Kindle, Barnes & Noble Nook e-reader, Apple iPad and other tablets, the eBook industry continues to grow and prosper, and offers a tremendous opportunity for indie authors, marketers and more.

You might have heard the term, "everyone has a book in them." It may be true that we all have potential novels in us, but the chances of writing a successful novel are very remote. It takes great imagination and writing talent to be a successful novelist. However, self-publishing is making it possible for anyone to publish their own books, and some with great success.

The real opportunity is in the non-fiction book genre addressing people's need for accurate, concise and valuable information. The self-help and information product market has existed for many, many years -- but marketplaces like Amazon.com, Nook, iBooks, KOBO and others are making it easier for buyers to find eBooks on every subject you can imagine.

Amazon.com alone has over 300 million active customers purchasing books, eBooks, electronics and more every single day.

Selling eBooks on Amazon is like putting your sales on auto-pilot. If you write an eBook that provides value for a reader, answers their questions on a topic, teaches them how to achieve success, or helps to fulfill a need that they have -- then your book can be successful.

Of course, success is a subjective term, but it is quite possible to sell hundreds of books per month with very little effort (after writing, creating and uploading the book) once your book is available for sale on one or all of these popular marketplaces.

There are two approaches to be a successful eBook author, in my opinion. You can write eBooks on topics that you have experience or expertise in -- where you want to share your knowledge. Or, you can research niche topics which sell the best and write eBooks on these topics (purely to make a profit).

However you come up with your topics, your goal will be to produce a well-written, well-researched "how-to" guide that satisfies the reader's interests and teaches them what they need to know about a particular topic.

Four areas of high interest for eBooks include weight loss, cooking, relationships and self-help. Self-help can include a wide variety of topics such as how to make money, how to be successful, and generally how to improve yourself in some specific area. Visit the Amazon.com Kindle Store to get an idea of some of the categories of eBooks available for purchase.

Your first step will be to figure out what topic you will write about. As I mentioned earlier, if you have experiences to share or expertise in a particular topic, then this is a logical starting point. Taking the other approach, you could research niche topics to determine what you will write about.

After you decide, you will want to develop an outline, and figure out what aspects of the topic you will focus on. Break it down into chapters and ensure it flows well. Next you will most likely need to do some research on the topic, or you may decide to start writing to get your own thoughts down on the page first.

I have read many books on the subject of writing and selling eBooks, and information products. In fact, there are numerous Kindle eBooks on the subject -- including *How to Write a Book in 7 Days* and many others.

Once your book is finished, and edited (very important), you must format it correctly (which can be a little tricky) and convert it to into various file formats, depending on which marketplaces you intend to utilize (.epub for KOBO, NOOK, and iBooks or .mobi for Amazon Kindle). Once converted, and tested, you are ready to upload the file to Amazon and/or other platforms for sale.

If you don't feel confident doing the formatting and conversion yourself, you can find individuals, virtual assistants and even eBook publishers that will do this for you for a fee (anywhere from $50 - $150). Search for these services online, but make sure to check their portfolio of previous clients.

I have been involved in the eBook industry since early 2012. My focus is on small business topics. I help readers learn about starting their own business, social media marketing and other small business topics. This is where my education, experience and skill set are strongest, and I always try to share useful tips, advice and strategies for success.

There are many tips I could offer about writing and selling eBooks that I have learned myself (or you can watch an Ignite Talk I did on the subject of self-publishing, several years ago at https://youtu.be/91PCkEJ77fQ).

One of the most important tips is to always have a high-quality cover for your book. It amazes me how many eBooks have cheap looking, low-quality covers. Selling your eBook online is like having a traditional book on a shelf at your local book store. The book cover is typically what draws someone to the book in the first place, and it is the same online.

Make sure that your eBooks have professional looking covers -- whether you make them yourself or you have a graphic designer create them (check out www.fiverr.com for some affordable options). This is one of the most important things you can do to ensure your success. Remember, you want people to find your book and purchase it online -- from that point, it is the content that will determine whether the customer will be pleased or not with their purchase.

Self-published eBooks typically are priced between $0.99 and $9.99, with the majority between $0.99 and $3.99. The higher the price, the more challenging it will be to compete with books from traditional publishers or established authors.

How much can you expect to make by selling eBooks? Every platform is different, but Amazon.com pays 35% commissions on eBooks priced between $0.99 and $2.98. They increase this to 70% for eBooks priced above $2.99. Obviously, it makes sense to sell your eBooks for $2.99 or more, but the eBook market is very competitive, and your book must provide enough value to justify the price, or it simply won't sell.

With just one or two semi-successful eBooks, you might expect to sell between 100-300 eBooks per month. Depending on the sale price, your monthly income in this scenario could be anywhere from $35 - $600! Not bad for a part-time business venture. Of course, the more eBooks you publish and the more successful each book is, the more money you will earn. There are many examples of successful indie authors, perhaps you will be one of them!

Marketing of eBooks is an entire topic on its own, but I can tell you that most authors utilize social media to promote their eBooks. You can promote your books on Twitter, Facebook, LinkedIn and other eBook promotion websites. Facebook has numerous groups where you can promote your eBooks.

You might also decide to use traditional marketing such as press releases, flyers, post cards and advertising. In most cases, however, if you are selling your eBook for just a few dollars, it might not justify the expense of some traditional advertising -- thus your main focus is typically online promotion.

From my experience, Amazon.com is the most profitable platform to sell your books. Their Kindle Direct Publishing (KDP) program also offers some benefits to new authors. By signing up with KDP, you agree to sell your eBook exclusively on Amazon for 90 days and in exchange, you are allowed 5 free days (where you can give your book away to grow your readership), and your book will be included in the Amazon Prime program, where members can borrow one eBook per month.

Amazon compensates authors of borrowed books by paying them from a monthly fund (at one time compensation was about $2 per borrow but is now calculated based on how many pages the borrower actually reads).

Since Amazon is by far the largest and most popular marketplace for eBooks, KDP is a good option for most eBook authors. I recommend you compare the options available.

Below is a list of resources for further information:

28 Resources, Tools & Tips for Self-Publishing Your Book
www.thewritelife.com/28-resources-tools-and-tips-for-self-publishing/

Amazon Kindle Direct Publishing
https://kdp.amazon.com/en_US

Publish and Sell Books on the iBooks Store
https://support.apple.com/en-us/HT201183

Video Production Business

Video as a medium continues to grow in popularity, and has become more personal with YouTube, Vlogging (video blogging), and other video apps on smartphones. Today the idea of making it big or gaining a lot of attention from videos is a reality.

Utilizing YouTube, Instagram and other tools to promote your business is a bonafide social media strategy. But businesses are still looking to have professional videos created, to promote their business, enhance their brand and to connect with a younger generation of consumers.

Creating marketing and promotional videos, and corporate training videos is a lucrative business that can be operated by one individual, even out of your home.

To capitalize on this opportunity, you must have some video production skills, the right equipment, and of course creativity. In this business, getting the shot is only half of the battle. The majority of the work takes place at your computer -- using popular software like Adobe Premiere or Final Cut Pro (MAC) to cut together all of the footage, insert transitions, music and voiceovers, text and other elements.

A typical videographer making corporate videos will require multiple pieces of equipment in order to deliver a top product. These include a high-quality video camera, or digital (DSLR) camera with video capabilities -- such as the Canon EOS 80D, which has a high pixel resolution and excellent video quality. Additional lenses are often required as well, for added flexibility.

You may also require other equipment such as wireless microphones, lighting equipment, and shades, a high-performance PC or MAC for processing the videos, and as previously mentioned, software to create your masterpiece.

This can quickly become one of the more expensive businesses mentioned in this book, however, as many videographers are enthusiasts, they tend to justify the purchase of high quality equipment, as they often use it for both business and personal use.

You might expect to pay anywhere from $2,000 - $6,000+ for a professional quality camera and lenses (although you may start your business with lower quality equipment). If you already have a solid PC or MAC, you may not need to buy a new one, however, you will need to purchase the necessary software which can run between $300 - $1,000.

Additional lighting, microphones, tripods etc. can cost anywhere from $500 - $1,500, and maybe less if you purchase used equipment.

What can you expect to make in this business? I know individuals who run this type of business in their spare time (although it can be a big-time commitment to complete each project) and charge anywhere from $2,000 - $10,000+ per project depending on the time required to film, complete interviews etc. and then associated production time.

In this business, you can quickly recoup your equipment costs, and then the main cost is your time. It is important when bidding on a project or providing a quote to a client, that you budget accurately for the time involved. Most videographers will budget based on a fixed hourly wage, which can make things easier.

Another added bonus for this type of business is that not only can your equipment be depreciated and written off as a business expense, but often times you can rent out your equipment to other videographers or filmmakers in your area.

Videographers I know have charged $500 per day to rent out their particular video cameras, and these are accepted rates you will find everywhere. Do a Google search for "rent video equipment NYC or Toronto" and you will see some of the daily and weekly rental costs for yourself.

This can be a great business to operate full-time or even part-time, especially if you have the passion for creative projects and of course the videography and software editing skills required.

You can find a lot of information online about the best equipment to use, video production techniques, tutorials and much more. I advise you to check out YouTube and Google for more information. You might want to pick up the latest issue of VideoMaker or other magazines at your local newsstand.

Alternatively, check your local college for continuing education courses in video production. It might be the kick start you need.

For more information, check out these sites:

Videomaker Magazine eNews
www.videomaker.com

How to Start a Video Production Company from Zero
http://1kcreatives.com/start-video-production-company-zero/

Making Money - Building a $1,000,000+ Video Production Company (YouTube)
www.youtube.com/watch?v=wP6xSaNEetY

Cupcake or Cake Business

Do you love to bake? Are you creative and have the skills to make works of art in the kitchen? Want to start a fun and delicious home business?

Custom cakes and cupcakes are big business. So big and popular, they have spawned their own reality television shows. But these yummy treats can no longer just taste great; they must look great too.

To be successful in this business is as much about design and artistic ability as it is about mixing the right ingredients. To excel and gain clients you will need a portfolio to show off your best work. This might include examples of birthday cakes, other themed cakes and cupcakes.

The perfect medium to showcase your work would be your own website or blog. Make sure to list your contact information and any other relevant details about your business. Utilize Pinterest, Facebook and Twitter to promote your business and share pictures of your latest work.

It is important for your business to offer a regular menu of items, as well as specializing in particular flavors or kinds of cakes and cupcakes. Custom orders can also be profitable.

The largest cost in running this type of business is typically the cost of the ingredients themselves. If you are operating out of your home, you will already most likely have an oven, mixer, measuring cups and other necessary items. You may, however, need to purchase several cupcake or cake pans and other specialized tools.

Check to see if there is a wholesale restaurant supply store in your area or purchase bulk ingredients at Costco and other bulk food stores to cut down on costs.

Make sure to check local regulations for food preparation businesses. Your home may require a visit by a local health inspector. Check with your municipality for details.

There are a lot of cookbooks and monthly magazines that can give you plenty of ideas for making cakes and cupcakes. Check your local library, bookstore or Amazon.com to see what is available.

Visit these websites for more information, tips and ideas:

Start a Cupcake Business
http://cupcake-business.com

7 Business Lessons from Gourmet Cupcakes
www.forbes.com/sites/allbusiness/2013/09/30/7-business-lessons-from-gourmet-cupcakes

Virtual Assistant

A virtual assistant (VA) is an independent contractor who provides administrative, technical or creative services remotely. VA's are usually hired by businesses and professionals in need of help or specific skills. Communication is typically via email, online chatting or the telephone.

Utilizing VA's can save businesses considerable expense such as office space, equipment costs, vacation and benefit costs, etc. which is helping to fuel the growth of this industry. Additionally, employers are billed only for the work that is completed, making VA's a very affordable alternative to additional employees.

The VA provides value by allowing companies to focus on the important aspects of their business, while delegating particular assignments and projects to the VA.

Becoming a virtual assistant might be the perfect fit for individuals with administrative experience, skills such as graphic design, web development, research, writing and communications skills. You can work with clients from around the world, in the comfort of your own home.

As a virtual assistant, you can have the ability to choose the type of work you are most interested in. When promoting your services, you can highlight specific specialties and experience that may qualify you for work that other's might not, but most VA's will typically provide a base level of administrative services as well.

Many virtual assistants I have come across offer general administrative as well as specialized skills such as eBook formatting or cover design. The ability to offer specialized skills can set you apart or allow you to focus on a niche market.

An article on Entrepreneur.com listed 10 popular tasks for outsourcing to virtual assistants: bookkeeping, online research, database entry, data presentations, managing email, social tasks, travel research, scheduling, chasing business and industry knowledge prep. You can read the article by visiting the following link: www.entrepreneur.com/article/225318

As with any profession, experience requirements in this industry vary, but most VA's have several years of experience in their particular specialty.

You can find work as a virtual assistant through websites like www.Upwork.com which matches freelancers and employers. You can create a profile listing your skills, experience and required wages, and employers can contact you directly. These sites also track the number of jobs you have completed and provide additional benefits for businesses, to make the process easier and reliable.

Many virtual assistants also have their own websites and promote their services using social media and other web marketing. Wages typically range from $5 - $50 per hour, depending on the level of skill and experience as well as location of the individual.

There are numerous websites, and associations which provide more details about becoming a virtual assistant as well as offering training programs.

To read about one busy executive's experience using a virtual assistant, visit the link: www.michaelhyatt.com/my-experience-using-a-virtual-assistant.html

For more information, visit these websites:

Canadian Association of Virtual Assistant –
https://canadianava.org/

International Virtual Assistants Association - www.ivaa.org

Photography Business

Photography is a great business for creative people. It is something that takes skill and experience but can definitely be learned. With a modest investment in a good DSLR camera, a few different lenses, and some lighting/flash equipment ($500-3,000) you will be ready for business.

It is a good idea to read as many books and magazines on photography as you can to learn the ins-and-outs of taking different types of pictures and the camera settings that will be needed to achieve the best possible shots. And of course, get out there and practice!

The main clients or jobs for this type of business will include family portraits, weddings, baby portraits, business events and possibly even news coverage (freelance work). Because the majority of the jobs you book will be very important events for the clients, you must ensure that you have the necessary skills and practice to deliver quality work. The last thing you want is for the client to be unhappy with the shots -- imagine the devastation if a newlywed couple's wedding photos did not turn out well!

Good photographers can be hard to find, and word-of-mouth will spread quickly if you do a great job (and maybe more quickly if you don't). I know several people who have started out part-time and then quit their full-time jobs because their businesses have grown so fast. This is one business where talent and creativity will pay dividends!

One of the things that sets photographers apart from each other is the use of creativity in their shots. Don't be afraid to step out of the box. One entrepreneurial photographer I know has made a name for himself because he takes a lot of non-traditional photos -- and the result is fun, exciting and interesting looking photos. Because of his unique style, his business has grown tremendously due to word-of-mouth and social media.

This photographer posts preview shots on his blog and shares them through social media like Facebook and Twitter, garnering a lot of comments and views along the way.

Having the photography skills is one aspect of the business, but as mentioned above, it will be important to promote and showcase your work to build your client base. At a bare minimum you should have a blog or website where you can post your work, along with information about your style or techniques, pricing and available packages. Provide contact information and encourage clients to contact you as soon as possible to book dates.

Most photographers ask for a deposit up-front to reserve a date (especially weddings). This is a good practice, because you don't want to turn down a job because you are already booked, only to have the existing client cancel. Requiring a deposit usually ensures that only serious clients book your time.

Visit these websites for more information, tips and ideas:

Video Photography Studio – Tips and resources
http://virtualphotographystudio.com/photographyblog

How to Start a Photography Business
https://photographyspark.com/how-to-start-a-photography-business/

Freelance Writing Business

If you are a gifted writer, with the skills to write different kinds of content, then a freelance writing business could be a good fit for you. Everything from news articles and product reviews on websites and blogs, to marketing materials for small businesses could be possible.

Local news publications or websites in your area could be potential clients for your business as well as blogs or magazines -- since they are in the business of providing content to their subscribers.

Consider reaching out to your local college/university that publishes an alumni magazine or offer to write a column for a local free newspaper.

Build a portfolio of your writing samples or start your own blog to showcase your work, then contact these companies. Try pitching specific ideas for articles and then direct them to your samples for further evidence of your writing abilities.

Typically, all that is needed for this type of business is a laptop or tablet, with printer and Internet access, and a word processor app or software. If you will be doing interviews you may wish to purchase a small tape recorder or use your smartphone with an external microphone.

Marketing this type of service will be very targeted -- send writing samples along with your story ideas directly to the editors of blogs, websites or newspapers. Offer to write a guest post on a popular blog to increase your exposure and deliver some traffic back to your own website.

Don't be afraid to volunteer your services for free in order to build your portfolio.

Your website or blog should have all of your writing samples, as well as content to show your expertise. Build your social media presence so that you can share your work and drive traffic.

Offer your writing services to local companies and contact others online. Companies are often in need of writing services, newsletter development, annual reports and more.

Businesses and organizations can find it challenging to dedicate the resources to develop new information, customer stories or content for their websites -- they might just be looking for someone with your skills.

Ask existing and past clients for referrals. Use Facebook and LinkedIn to promote your business and showcase your work. Facebook and Google Ads can also be effective in promoting your freelancing. Ask your past clients to provide endorsements and recommendations on LinkedIn. Providing social proof can be quite powerful.

Freelance writing can be a very rewarding business. You will be involved in a variety of projects and write about a great variety of topics. You may also choose to focus on particular niche areas -- such as corporate communications or the fitness industry if that is where your interest or experience lies.

Visit these websites for more information, tips and ideas:

How to Start a Freelance Writing Business
www.thebalancesmb.com/home-business-idea-freelance-writer-1794506

Complete Guide to Getting Started in Freelance Writing
https://elnacain.com/blog/getting-started-freelance-writing/

House Cleaning Business

Society continues to change, people are busier, and in many families both parents work full-time. With our hectic lifestyles, people want to enjoy their free time to relax, spend with family or take part in other activities. But housework and cleaning still need to get done.

Many people choose to utilize house cleaning services on a regular basis - whether it be weekly, bi-weekly or even monthly.

This presents an opportunity. This type of business can be started with very little cost. Cleaning supplies (many clients provide their own cleaning supplies) and some advertising are all that are required. Although this business is heavily driven by word-of-mouth, in the beginning some classified advertising, flyers and other low-cost methods can help drum up business.

Because the job is labor intensive, and will require driving to multiple locations, scheduling and time management are important and a vehicle will most likely be required.

Of course, it is important that you know how to clean properly and thoroughly, but chances are you have plenty of experience at home. Do a good job and clients will be consistent and reliable.

Ever since my daughter was born (5 years ago), we have utilized house cleaning services. When you realize the amount of time saved and the joy of coming home to a clean house, it is hard to go back! We have been lucky to find excellent house cleaners, but it can be difficult. Many are booked solid, and most people rely heavily on recommendations from friends and family to find a good match.

Because house cleaning often takes place while the owners are away, trust is a big part of this type of business. Being professional (not snooping or stealing) is obviously an important part of being successful in this industry. In some cases, you may need to be "bonded" and insured before clients will work with you.

Before you start promoting your business, determine what wage you will charge, for example $20-30 per hour. Make sure your wage is priced well for the market yet worthwhile for you personally and would also be enough to cover wages if you hire staff.

Don't be surprised if you find yourself with too many clients, and not enough time! This service business is in high demand, and if you do good work, you should have no problem at all finding clients.

As your business and reputation grow, there may be additional opportunities to branch into office cleaning or industrial cleaning.

Visit these websites for more information, tips and ideas:

How to Start a Cleaning Business
www.entrepreneur.com/article/41426

How to Start a House Cleaning Business
www.wikihow.com/Start-a-House-Cleaning-Business

How to Start a Residential House Cleaning Service
www.homebiztools.com/ideas/residential_cleaning.htm

CHAPTER 3 - MARKET RESEARCH

Coming up with an idea is only the first step. Business ideas need to be vetted through research to ensure they represent true opportunities.

Performing market research is an important step in the process of starting a business. Gut feelings aren't always enough to ensure your future success, although many entrepreneurs still rely on them! You need supporting data. To determine if there is a large enough market for your product or service, you will need to take a look at your proposed market.

According to www.entrepreneur.com market research is defined as *"The process of gathering, analyzing and interpreting information about a market, about a product or service to be offered for sale in that market, and about the past, present and potential customers for the product or service; research into the characteristics, spending habits, location and needs of your business's target market, the industry as a whole, and the particular competitors you face."*[4]

Market research can be made up of both primary and secondary research. Primary research comes from information and data you collect yourself such as through a survey, online tracking, and the feedback from real customers. Secondary research involves finding information that already exists and may include government reports (such as census demographics, and other statistics), industry data and forecasts, competitive intelligence (such as prices charged by the competition) and much more.

Most of the market research you will complete will be secondary information. Scour the Internet for information on your proposed business. You will find an incredible amount of useful information that you can use to determine if your idea can be successful.

For local markets, primary research becomes very important. Performing surveys, counting traffic at a location, and checking out the competition first hand are all examples of primary research. Using social media and other tools, it is becoming much easier and cheaper to communicate with your target market in real-time.

With Facebook ads, for example, you can target users that meet certain criteria, including sex, age, education level, interests and hobbies. If your ideal customer is a 35-year-old woman in New York, who is a foodie and enjoys watching the Cooking Channel, you can target those customers who meet that criteria and already like the Cooking Channel Facebook page. Now you just need to create a Facebook ad that will entice these prospects to click through and fill out your online survey.

Having the ability to ask your target market directly to determine if there is a need for your product or service, how often they would expect to use it, and the price they are willing to pay, would be invaluable.

Online tools like www.surveymonkey.com make it very easy to develop online surveys for market research. The survey results are automatically tabulated and results delivered in the form of charts and graphs for easy use in presentations or your business plan.

Additionally, many successful entrepreneurs subscribe to the "lean startup" methodology, where you develop a working product and release it "into the wild" to get feedback directly from users. The feedback is used to improve the product and make it better. In other words, develop your product in the least amount of time and expense, and then find out directly if customers will pay for the product and what features they would like to see. This is an example of primary research and is especially applicable to online products and services.

I had the opportunity to utilize an online survey program while completing a consulting project for a local client. The study investigated the feasibility of opening a small business incubator and co-working space in the community. Through the client I was able to email the survey to thousands of local businesses and entrepreneurs through their business directory, soliciting participation in a survey I had created for the project.

Hundreds of survey responses later, the results were both enlightening and valuable. Because I used the service, www.surveymonkey.com to carry out the survey, the whole process was automated, and results tallied for me. The finished product included a PDF report with responses and charts for every question. and the results confirmed that there was demand for the facility.

Assessing your Potential Target Market

Is your market local, regional, national or international? How do you plan to reach and or sell to this market?

How big is your potential market? If you said that your market is the city you live in and surrounding area, you might think your market is the population there – let's say 200,000 people. But is the entire population really interested in your product or service? The answer is probably no.

To better answer the question, you must first identify who your customer really is. Try to visualize what your ideal customer might look like and the qualities they might have in common (demographics). Maybe your ideal customer is a male, aged 20-39 and is interested in technology and gadgets. Is your target market still 200,000 people? No. As a matter of fact, your actual potential market has shrunk significantly. Perhaps it is now just 30,000. Is this enough to support your business? What percentage of that 30,000 do you expect to convert to paying customers? This will depend on many factors, including competition.

These are just some of the questions you need to ask yourself. Other factors to consider include education levels, household income, and possibly even religion or culture. Depending on your product or service, your target market may be very specific, or a niche market.

Once you have determined who your target market is, you can determine the size of your market locally, regionally or nationally using census data from Statistics Canada or the U.S. Census Bureau. To narrow it down even further, Canada Post and the U.S. Postal Service have tools available which break down the demographics of the population by postal code or zip code. For example, this information could identify income levels by postal or zip code. This can be very useful for direct mail marketing or determining the best location for your business.

Once you determine who your target customer is, the challenge will be how to reach them most effectively within your budget. More on this in chapter 8.

For more information on market research visit these websites:

www.sba.gov/business-guide/plan-your-business/market-research-competitive-analysis

www.canadabusiness.ca/eng/page/2829/

www.canadabusiness.ca/business-planning/market-research-and-statistics/conducting-market-research/guide-to-market-research-and-analysis/

www.census.gov

Industry Trends

"Understanding trends specific to your industry can help you plan and predict the future."[5] So as you are researching your potential business, look at where the industry has moved over the last 5-10 years, and where it is heading. In some industries such as with cellular phones or personal computers it may have changed dramatically. Not recognizing these changes could mean the difference between success and failure, even for established companies.

Let's take a look at a real-world example:

Blackberry (formerly Research in Motion or RIM) is the maker of the Blackberry smartphone and creator of wireless email. RIM practically invented the smartphone industry and its devices were once so popular they were nicknamed "Crackberry". RIM had created the remarkable device with best-in-class wireless email, an unsurpassed physical keyboard, and free text messaging through Blackberry Messenger. RIM grew at an astounding rate as the company innovated and its products became ubiquitous with business professionals throughout the world.

Blackberry began to gain popularity with consumers as well, helping RIM to grow revenues very quickly. Then Apple changed everything with the launch of the iPhone in 2007. Not only did the new touch screen smartphone blindside RIM and other competitors, but RIM dismissed the iPhone as a "toy".

As the iPhone grew in popularity, RIM attempted to follow suit, adding touch screen capabilities and even launched a full touch screen device which was plagued with problems, bad reviews and was a market bomb.

Today, iPhone is on its 8th iteration, and selling more units than ever. Blackberry on the other hand, has just completed a pivot from hardware producer to a software company. The company no longer produces Blackberry smartphones, but rather licenses the technology to several companies that are producing phones under the Blackberry Mobile brand. While they may have come out of their death spiral, revenues have dropped from their peak of $20.6 billion in 2011 to just $1.3 billion in 2017.

Apple iPhone and Android smartphones have crushed the competition over the last five years, and at last count Blackberry market share was less than 0.1%. Meanwhile, Apple has sold more than 1 billion iPhones since 2007.

The lesson learned is that technology can disrupt entire industries quickly. Innovation can lead to new products and the death of previous cutting-edge technology. Even successful companies need to monitor where the industry is moving and take appropriate action to stay relevant.

When researching your business idea, it is important to understand industry trends, so you don't spend your time or money investing in a product or service that is on its way out.

A good way to find information on trends and developments in the industry or sector you are considering is to monitor company news reports, follow industry blogs, and search for industry forecasts online. Follow the leading companies in the space, the ones that are driving the industry growth and development.

Assessing the Competition

Unless your product or service is totally unique, the chances of having absolutely no competition are very slim. There will most likely be other businesses selling similar products or offering the same or similar services.

It is important to identify these competitors and learn everything you can about them. What will set your business apart? What is your strategy to compete? Lower prices? Better customer service?

The easiest way to identify potential competitors is to do an online search or look in the yellow pages (for local competition). Maybe you decide to start a carpet cleaning business. If you look in the local yellow pages there may be 10 carpet cleaning businesses listed. That is 10 local competitors which your business must compete with. A quick Google search could also identify others.

You can continue your research by visiting each competitor's website or calling directly to get prices and the specifics of what they offer. This information becomes very useful and can help you to determine if your market is big enough to ensure success. The pie is only so big and with so many slices already taken, is the remainder enough for your business?

Identifying the prices charged by competitors will also be valuable when assessing your idea and writing your business plan. If all your competitors are charging similar prices, then it may be difficult to charge more in that particular market. Can your business be profitable by charging "the going rate"? Also, if this is the case, then your business needs to compete on something other than price. What will differentiate your business from the competition?

Researching your competitors can also help you identify best practices and service standards for running a particular type of business or provide other ideas you may not have thought of.

Make sure to do a thorough analysis of the competition, and don't forget about indirect competition (often called substitutions). While operating my computer camps business, for several years there were no direct competitors, however, indirectly we had a lot of competition for our campers from other sports camps, science camps, and summer programs. Thus, we had to consider the pricing for alternative summer camps as well, even though there were no other computer camps in the area.

Finding your Niche

Focusing on a specific portion of a market can prove to be a very successful strategy. When Amazon.com launched in 1995, it focused strictly on selling books. Its goal was to be the largest bookseller in the world -- by having the largest selection of books possible. Amazon.com succeeded, and eventually expanded its product lines to include many kinds of merchandise such as computers, electronics, appliances, clothing and more.

If Amazon.com had originally launched itself as an online retailer offering such a wide variety of products it may not have been as successful as it has been, and in fact may not have survived at all. By focusing on books, Amazon.com was able to focus on its target market, and develop its business into an efficient consumer-centric product distribution business. By developing a loyal customer base and being good at what it does, Amazon.com was able to continue growing the business and its reputation as a fantastic online retailer. Adding new products to their mix became a natural extension of the business.

Local Sources of information

The Internet is probably the most efficient source of information these days. But don't discount some of the more traditional sources. Make sure to tap local free business advisory services also – most communities or government agencies offer advice, support and small business programs.

Other sources include:

- Local economic development or small business agencies
- Local public library, college or university library
- Business periodicals or trade publications
- Encyclopedia of Associations (Gale Research)
- Competitor websites, annual reports and industry information
- Chamber of Commerce and other development agencies
- Canada Post and the U.S. Postal Service have demographic information about everyone living in a particular Postal Code or Zip Code. This can be extremely useful in identifying where your customers live.

Additional Resources

U.S. Census Bureau

U.S. Small Business Administration

Business and Industry Canada

U.S. Government Bookstore

CHAPTER 4 - THE BUSINESS PLAN

Business planning may be one of the least favorite activities for potential entrepreneurs, but it continues to be one of the most important things you can do to help ensure your success.

We have already spoken about fleshing out your ideas to ensure they have a potential market. The business plan is the next step to ensure the business itself is feasible. By putting your ideas down on paper, you will force yourself to think about, and clarify your business proposition. A business plan will show the bank, investors, clients and even potential partners that your business can work based on your assumptions.

The business plan will outline your business concept, provide an overview of the industry and market, explain how the business will operate, describe how you intend to market your products or services, discuss the opportunities and risks involved, identify financing requirements and much more.

There has been much discussion about the need for formal business plans today. We are seeing a shift to other tools and models that allow entrepreneurs to rapidly launch and evolve their businesses.

In the next chapter we will hear from Bob Minhas, the Founder of Entrepreneur House and his thoughts on business planning. But one thing can be argued about business plans -- banks and other funders still want to see them before they lend to a business.

Components of a Business Plan

Depending on your needs, a business plan can be lengthy and very detailed, or it can be very simple. Most traditional business plans contain the following components:

1. **Cover Page** - Includes your company's name, address, telephone number, website address, email address and your name.

2. **Table of Contents** - Number each page and ensure each section of the plan has a title. Then create a table of contents. This will allow readers to quickly flip to a specific part of the plan.

3. **Executive Summary** - This is the most important part of the business plan. Most readers will only spend a few minutes looking over the business plan. A well written executive summary should introduce the reader to the business concept and convince him or her that the business can be successful. It should summarize the most important points of each section of your plan.

The executive summary should be written after completing the rest of the plan, to capture the most important information.

4. **Company Description and History** - Briefly describe the business, including company objectives and milestones achieved. An established business should provide a brief history of the company, its structure and any key information. If it is a new or proposed business you will focus on the structure the business will take, and what has led up to the development of the idea.

5. **Industry and Market Analysis** - Discuss your industry, including trends and opportunities. This will include an

industry description and outlook. Next, describe your target market, and market size. Perform a competitive analysis where you will discuss your direct and indirect competition. Many plans will include a SWOT analysis, which looks at the strengths, weaknesses, opportunities and threats of the business.

Make sure to include a summary of the market research you have performed or gathered.

6. **Product or Service Description** - Describe what your business offers. Discuss the products or services offered and what makes them different from the competition. You will also describe your pricing strategy, and how your business will be positioned in the market.

7. **Marketing Plan** - Describe how you intend to reach your target market through specific advertising, promotion and marketing efforts. Also include your sales strategy in this section. Provide specific information about the company's sales activities, strategic partnerships and special promotions.

8. **Operational Plan** - Describe how the business operates in terms of acquiring or producing its products, and how the products will be distributed. Include information on the company's facilities, location and other operational details like order fulfillment and customer service.

9. **Management Team** - Explain how your skills, knowledge and experience will make the business successful. If there are employees or partners, describe their skill sets and what they bring to the table. Depending on your business, you may be the only employee. Sell yourself, and why you have the right background to build the company.

10. **Financial Plan** - This can be the most challenging portion of the business plan. Investors and banks typically look for 3-5 years of projected cash-flow statements, income statements and balance sheets. If you haven't started the business, then this information will be based on your research, expected sales and associated costs of running the business.

It is better to be conservative and show a realistic startup scenario. Sometimes it is useful to produce a best-case, normal-case and worst-case scenario to demonstrate whether the business is still viable if sales are not as expected.

11. **Appendices** - In the appendices of the business plan, you may wish to include other documentation such as the resumes of key personnel, the results of market surveys or other research, examples of marketing and promotional material, even letters-of-intent from potential customers.

Business Planning Resources

The business plan is a key document for any business. But, due to the perceived difficulty and amount of work involved, it can be very intimidating to new entrepreneurs.

The advice I would give is to start with a plan, whether it is a full-blown formal business plan or a very simple plan outlining your ideas. The level of formality usually depends on whether you will be seeking financing.

Newer alternatives to the traditional business plan include one-page business plans and the Business Model Canvas. More on this in the next chapter.

Regardless of the format used, the process of writing the plan will help you to solidify your ideas and help you to communicate what you are proposing. I have provided a list of resources below, to help you learn more about business planning and to make available various templates you can use to speed up the process:

[Create the Plan — RBC Royal Bank](#)

[BDC Entrepreneur's Toolkit](#)

[U.S. Small Business Administration](#)

Sample Plans – [www.bplans.com/sample_business_plans.php](#)

[www.liveplan.com/](#)

Financial Analysis

While working with clients to develop their plans, perhaps the area where the most clients struggled was with the financial statements. After all, how can you project what your sales revenues, expenses or profits will be over the next three years when you haven't even started the business?

It may sound impossible, but you must start somewhere. This is where your research comes into play.

One of the first steps will be to determine the startup costs of the business. Grab a notepad or open your spreadsheet software and start listing everything you will need to purchase or pay for in order to launch your business. This could include computer equipment, software, insurance, rent, utilities, furniture, legal costs, advertising, wages and much more.

After you have come up with your list, estimate how much each item will cost. For example, you may be required to pay the first and last month of rent in your retail space or outfit the space with new office furniture. These expenses should be verified through your research.

Below is an example of what your startup costs (budget) might look like:

Company XYZ Startup Cost Estimate

Monthly Costs	
Salaries and wages	$3,000
Rent	1,000
Advertising	700
Internet	200
Supplies	200
Telephone	200
Other utilities	600
Insurance	250
Equipment lease	200
Interest	50
Legal and other professional fees	100
Miscellaneous	200
Subtotal	**$6,700**
One-Time Costs	
Fixtures and Equipment	5,000
Furniture	2,000
Deposits with public utilities	500
Legal and other professional fees	1,000
Software	1,500
Advertising and promotion for opening	2,000
Cash	4,000
Subtotal	**$16,000**
Totals	**$22,700**

According to this example, Company XYZ requires $22,700 in startup funds to cover both one-time costs and the first month of operations. Calculating the estimated startup costs will help you figure out how much money is required to start the business.

Determining the break-even point for your business can be very useful as it will tell you the point at which your revenues equal your fixed expenses. Any additional sales above that point will contribute to your profit.

This type of information is very valuable as you develop the business plan and operate the business. A simple example for a retail business is below:

Break-Even Point Example

Revenue per unit	$20
Cost per unit	12
Gross margin	8
Monthly expenses	
Rent	$1,000
Utilities	200
Insurance	100
Wages	4000
Supplies	500
Total fixed expenses	5,800

Break-even point= 5,800/$8 = 750 units

From this example, we can see that we need to sell 750 units per month just to cover the fixed costs of the business. Information like this will help you to determine if the business is feasible or not.

I will give you a real-world example from my Adventures in Computing camps business. In our second year of operation, one of our beginner camps was struggling with low enrolment. On the Friday before camp started, only five kids were enrolled (compared to 20 in most camps). We had to decide whether to offer the camp the following week. With only five registrations we were bound to lose money -- but how much?

Luckily, we had calculated our break-even point for that camp. At the time, this camp was priced at $169.95/week. Our fixed costs per week were $1,000 (essentially wages) because we had worked out a deal with the university for free computer lab space. With only five students, we stood to lose $150 for the week.

You can't operate your business at a loss for extended periods of time without risks, but since we were a new program and were not keen on cancelling any camps, we decided to offer the camp regardless of the small loss.

As it turned out, by Monday morning there were seven students enrolled which worked out to a profit of $190. My point is, it was important to understand what our break-even point was to make an informed decision.

Financial Statements

The three most common types of financial statements included in a business plan are the income statement, cash-flow statement, and balance sheet. Usually a bank or investor will want to see 3-5 years of forecasted financial statements.

Both the income statement and balance sheet are typically completed on an annual basis, while it is more likely that monthly cash-flow statements for the period will be required.

Below are more detailed explanations of each:

Income Statement - Shows a business' revenues and expenses over a specific period (usually monthly or annually). The income statement essentially shows if the business is making a profit.

Company XYZ Income Statement

Income statement for the year ended December 31, 2018	
Revenue	$65,000
Expenses	
Cost of goods sold	7,000
Rent	6,000
Wages	31,000
Office supplies	1,000
Total expenses	45,000
Net income	20,000

Cash-flow Statement - Shows the flow of cash in and out of the business over a specific period. Adequate cash-flow can make or break a business. Businesses often run into trouble because they do not have enough cash to pay their bills, because it is tied up in inventory or owed to the company by customers (accounts receivable). The cash-flow statement will show if the company has enough free cash to pay its bills.

Company XYZ Cash-flow Statement

Company XYZ
Cash-flow Statement
Year ended December 31, 2018

Net income	$20,000
	20,000
Cash from operating activities	
Decrease in Accounts Receivable	3,000
Increase in inventory	(5,000)
Increase in Accounts payable	2,000
Increase in Due to shareholder	3,000
	3,000
Cash from investing activities	
Purchase of capital assets	(5,000)
	(5,000)
Cash from financing activities	
Repayment of loans	(6,000)
	(6,000)
Total increase in cash	12,000
Opening cash balance	11,425
Closing cash balance	**$23,425**

Balance Sheet - Shows how much a company is worth at a specific moment in time (usually at year-end). The balance sheet shows what a company owns (assets), what it owes (liabilities) and the net worth of the company (owner's equity).

Because owner's equity represents the net worth of the business, an easy formula to remember is:

$$\text{Assets} - \text{Liabilities} = \text{Owner's equity}$$

Company XYZ Balance Sheet

Balance sheet as at December 31, 2018	
Assets	
Cash	23,425
Account receivable	3,000
Inventory	5,000
Capital assets	10,750
Total assets	**42,175**
Liabilities	
Current	
Accounts payable	2,000
Line of credit payable	1,950
Long term	
Equipment loan	3,900
Bank loan	8,500
Total liabilities	**16,350**
Owner's equity	
Retained earnings	25,725
Capital stock	100
Total owner's equity	**25,825**
Total liabilities and owner's equity	42,175

We've just gone through the process of learning to write a formal business plan. A plan which would normally be used to obtain financing for your business. But what if you don't need external financing or you need to move quickly to seize upon an opportunity?

We will explore some other options in the next chapter, but first, another perspective.

Business Plans: Old School or Necessity?

By Bob Minhas, Founder of Entrepreneur House

They're a necessity...But there's a twist.

Knowing how much money you have and how much you're going to need to start and maintain your business. Knowing who your target audience is and how you plan to reach them with marketing. Knowing how you plan to grow, and staff your business, how you plan to pay your staff and how you plan to manage your business during a crisis. These are all things that you probably know, as an entrepreneur, but having them in your head doesn't help you.

The argument has been made that in this day and age of rapid growth startups, a business plan is basically obsolete before you've finished writing it; that it sets up too many restrictions on the direction you take with your business, but I have to disagree with this view. Too many businesses are built on a wing and a prayer, without thought to the downstream effects. Success or failure for many of these businesses comes down to luck rather than strategy and that seems like a poor basis for long term growth to me.

Writing down your strategy doesn't confine you to that route but it puts all of your plans in context and makes it easier to get the perspectives of others, including mentors. Like it or not, most investors will want to see some form of a business plan, since looking into your head isn't really an option. A presentation à la Dragon's Den or Shark Tank isn't how you'll end up attracting interest in your business.

So, while the notion of a business plan may seem, on the surface, a static, stodgy old school tool, if executed in modern fashion, it's not.

What do I mean by 'modern fashion' business planning?

Don't get hung up on the 'how' of writing it: you're not going to win prizes for style, unless this activity is part of your MBA program. Instead, look at a plan as a fluid document, a representation of your business strategy and how you will get from your original thoughts to the final goals, an actionable view of what you're going to accomplish today, tomorrow and in the next five years. Rather than a historical document of the business model, a modern plan will be a work in progress; something that forces you to deliver on action items to move it forward.

Don't forget to think about quality over quantity. You need to get down some plans for real action items, but you don't need to graph your projected earnings for the next twenty years. Likely, your numbers would be as much a guess as anything else anyway. Don't waste your time.

What is essential for any business plan that will work for you?

1. Be clear about your vision. Write it down. Not how you're going to get there; that comes later. For now, you're looking at the end goal in your mind. What does it look like?

2. Before you move forward with your idea, you need to be sure that your model makes sense, that it's scalable, and that it is a business that can grow.

Build a Business Model Canvas — this is an invaluable tool to help you to design your business, innovate your ideas and, if necessary, change direction with your business model, quickly and easily. It gives you an essential view of parts of your business including:

- Costs – What are your startup expenses and ongoing costs?
- Revenue streams – How will you earn money?
- Customer groups – Who are we looking to buy from us?
- Resources / partners – Who do we need to help us make this work?
- Key activities – What is important to do right away?
- Value propositions – Why should those customer groups buy from us? What makes us special?

Create action items that will take you from your present to the future that you envisioned in step 1. Each one must be focused so that you stay on task. Imagination is a great thing, and you need to take the time to think outside the box, but at some point, you must get down to the business at hand in order to move forward. The action items will help you to remain focused and as they are completed, your fluid document is altered.

Why is it necessary to do future planning?

It might seem a step too far to be planning five years into the future, but the reality is that decisions you make today can affect the outcome, years down the line. Scalability of resources or machinery, for example. If you don't think about where you want to be in the future, you will make short term decisions now that could end up costing you more in the long run.

Just look at politics to get a sense of what I mean: politicians, who are elected to relatively short terms, are looking to make an impact now. Few look to how things should be in ten or twenty years. The decisions they make often reflect that view.

Future planning isn't about guessing at the projected revenues. It's about having the end goal in mind so that the decisions you make today will still make sense tomorrow. Mentors are a great way to find out if your idea has merit so get working on your plan and we can help you with the rest.

CHAPTER 5 – BUSINESS PLAN ALTERNATIVES

Over the last decade or so the task of business planning has evolved, and the traditional business plan has made way for alternatives that are faster and more relevant. It may no longer be the best option to spend months writing a business plan, when markets and opportunities are changing faster than ever.

In his article on www.inc.com, best-selling author and professor, Dr. Sean Wise provides an interesting perspective on how business planning has changed over the last 20 years:

"Business plans are dead. Business planning is alive and well. Two decades ago, I was taught to plan everything in advance, to write a perfect business plan, and only then go out into the world. This couldn't be further from the truth. The Lean Startup movement, which entered our zeitgeist around 2008, teaches that to be successful, entrepreneurs must 'get out of the building' and engage in customer discovery."

"Today, you must take your idea to market, and develop it through iteration and customer interaction. Startup founders who obsess over a detailed business plan prior to launch are missing the point. The best written business plans don't survive first contact with users. Startups are living things; business plans are static. Today, it is better to launch early and iterate often. A lean canvas beats a business plan."[6]

The One-Page Business Plan

As mentioned above, a popular methodology is called lean startup. Essentially it involves moving quickly to market without perfecting your product or service; then refining your offering based on customer feedback. This is common with Internet-based services and other digital products and services.

Often if the business idea does not require a lot of capital, and the risks associated with failure are low, then launching the business before embarking on a significant amount of market research, and financial analysis can make sense.

In this case a one-page business plan may be all you need, at least for the startup stage.

For his best-selling book, *The $100 Startup: Reinvent the Way You Make A Living, Do What You Love, and Create a New Future*, author Chris Guillebeau interviewed thousands of successful entrepreneurs who have started microbusinesses -- businesses they started for a couple hundred dollars. What he found is that many of the entrepreneurs followed a similar pattern, "Get started quickly and see what happens. There's nothing wrong with planning, but you can spend a lifetime making a plan that never turns into action. In the battle between planning and action, action wins."[7]

In other words, if you can start the business quickly, with very little capital (and risk), it might make sense to just start and see what happens. Is your promotional strategy working as planned? Have your customers and sales materialized? Evaluate the business as it operates and make tweaks as you go.

Guillebeau goes on to say, "In a microbusiness built on low costs and quick action, you don't need to do much formal planning."

So, whether you feel your business requires a formal business plan or a one-page business plan, the exercise of planning your business is still very important.

For more information on one-page business plans visit:

Keep It Simple: How To Write A One Page Business Plan
www.entrepreneurmag.co.za/advice/business-plans/how-to-guides-business-plans/keep-it-simple-how-to-write-a-one-page-business-plan/

Build a one-page business plan
www.theglobeandmail.com/report-on-business/small-business/sb-managing/build-a-one-page-business-plan/article4180506/

The One Page Business Plan – Sample Plan
http://images.oprah.com/download/pdfs/omag/omag_200709_businessplan_consulting.pdf

Business Model Canvas: A Deeper Dive

By Bob Minhas, Founder of Entrepreneur House

Business Model Canvas (BMC) is a tool for taking your concept from ideation to potential validation through the creation of a business model. Originally created by Alexander Osterwalder, it has since been revised several times and regurgitated in a number of different formats. The BMC works by essentially taking all of the variables that can impact your business idea and placing it in a visual format.

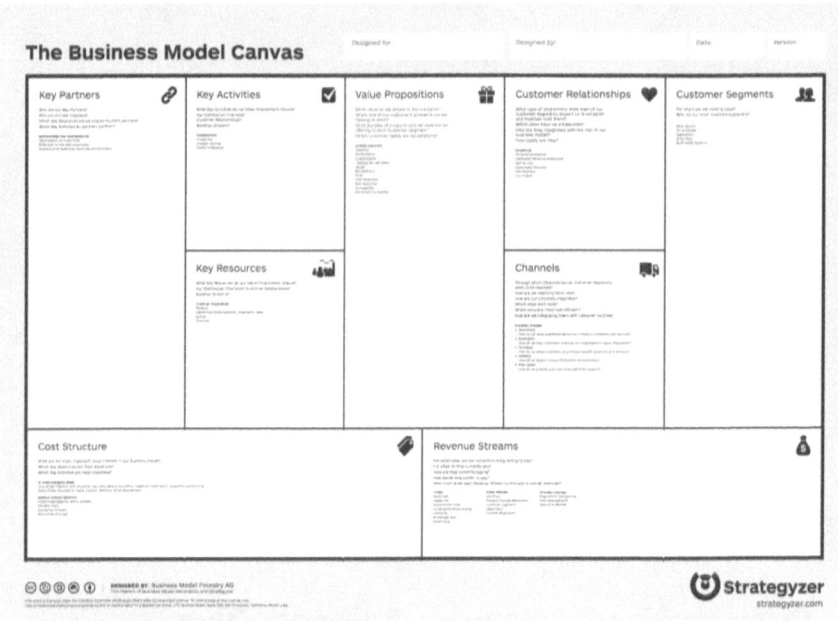

Business Model Canvas: nine business model building blocks,
Osterwalder, Pigneur & al. 2010 (Source: Wikipedia.org)

The BMC challenges you to ask uncomfortable or difficult questions about your idea. Who will want it? Why? What people do you need to make it happen? How much will it cost you? How much will you charge those who will want it? It's a 10,000 foot screenshot image of what your plan is. And it allows you to pivot and trade off as you need, while you adjust the "engine" of your idea.

The BMC is NOT a replacement for a traditional business plan. Rather it is a precursor to one. Before you write 80 pages, only to find that at page 81, that you now must go back to an earlier point in the business plan and make an adjustment impacting every other page after it…you want to ensure your information is on point. Know that from my experience in North America, any institution that is a financial lender will still expect to see a traditional business plan laid out when you ask for funding.

How does it work?

Keep in mind you can use the BMC in any way you feel comfortable. You can write within the columns or use sticky notes to add ideas. When I worked with an Artrepreneur cohort, there were students who actually drew their thoughts out on the BMC in picture format. However, you need to get what's in your head out on the page, and without a filter.

The BMC outlines nine key variables but is most effective when you start out by defining the Value Proposition (interchangeably used with the term Unique Selling Proposition) of your idea. The Value Proposition (VP) is the reason why a consumer should buy your product or service.

A VP requires some considerations. Do you have an original idea? How do you get people to take action on what you offer? Is your product/service similar to others on the market? Why are they choosing you over the competition? What is it about your idea that makes it a worthwhile concept? It's the same filter of judgment we all go through when meeting the parents of our significant other for the first time.

Often, when I speak to entrepreneurs about the concept of Value Proposition, I remind them that a VP can be like a truncated version of your Executive Summary in a traditional business plan. And in both cases, a Value Proposition resolves some sort of clear pain point for a segment of the population who you want to target for this idea. The deeper the pain, the more impactful your solution will be to them.

Pain points can be tough to dig into for some entrepreneurs who just start with an idea. So, when I work with entrepreneurs

I take them through two quick exercises to develop some sort of VP to start with. Remember as you develop the BMC you can come back and pivot based on what you've learned.

Try these two exercises to help craft your Value Proposition:

1. List three reasons why YOUR SOLUTION is the right idea for the market segment you want to target.

    a) Come up with three words that really identify why this is important. Is it cost accessible? Is it innovative (attracting early adopters)? Is it unique? Take those three words, and then lay it out in a sentence.

    b) Example. If I were to write: People engage me in coaching because I am "experienced" and I am "open-minded" and I am "creative" then I might write a VP that reads "I provide business coaching services in an open-minded environment and offer creative solutions that come from real experience."

2. The game of 5 Why's.

    Why are YOU doing this? What is it about you and your core values that make this something that should happen? This is about really digging into what drives you, which in turn will drive this idea. For some of you, you may find this is an exercise that works best with someone you trust asking the why. Again, going back to my business of coaching as an example:

    a) I am doing this because it's a need for small business owners. WHY?

    b) I am doing this because I know I needed it when I had my small business. WHY?

c) I am doing this because I felt alone in what I was doing in my small business. WHY?

d) I am doing this because I felt judged because I didn't know how to run my small business. WHY?

e) I am doing this because I am blessed to have more knowledge and experience in my business repertoire and I want to share it with others, so they don't have to feel as alone and scared as I did in their small business.

Now, taking the first iteration of the Value Proposition, and based on this exercise of 5 Why's above, I might change my VP to read: I want to help other small business owners feel in control of their success by giving them the tools I've learn to make my business successful.

You see how I went from a more professional, perhaps clinical VP to one which really tapped into the pain point of what I know my market segment is feeling? From here, building out the rest gets so much easier.

For the left side of the BMC, we're really thinking about operational questions.

Key Partnerships - The idea here is to describe who can make your business idea happen and continue to operate. Are these suppliers or funders? Who are the ongoing partners you need to maintain for success in your model? For example, in my coaching business, key partners would be accountants and bookkeepers. Who else could have great insights into a business owner struggling?

Another for me is often business bankers and financial institutions, as they provide a little deep level help in their consulting. A third would be government funded support agencies that offer high level business advice, but not deeper insights.

Key Activities - We all have so many amazing ideas. And there's nothing wrong with a business that might have multiple revenue streams. However, focus is very important to being able to execute your idea. So, you have to ask yourself, what are the one-to-three core products/services you'll offer? In my coaching business, I offer one-on-one coaching, but I also offer group coaching. More recently I've added online education as a third core activity. This works for me because they all align in what each offers and can actually act as a funnel/filter. I get people in my inexpensive online course. They grow their business and invest in group coaching and after some time might invest in one-on-one coaching for very specific needs within their business.

Key Resources - These are the actual resources that are integral to produce what you are offering. For a product, it might be the raw goods. For services it could be a professional designation or even a specific type of insurance. This resource is critical to the operation of your business. In my coaching business, a major key resource would be Errors and Omissions Insurance. Another would be an online platform with a subscription functionality such as Teachable.com for my online courses. A third could be Zoom.us for one-on-one coaching with remote clients. Without these elements, I could not effectively operate based on my core idea.

Now that we've talked about operations, let's chat about the right side of the canvas, which covers marketing.

Customer Relationships - This is where you want to really clarify what type of relationship you want to have with your client. This would be the segment of market that responds to the solutions you offer to their pain point. I usually like to start this section with emotion. How do you want customers to feel about your brand? What feeling does your brand offer them? More than just relief from their pain point, do they feel empowered, do they feel excited, do they feel victorious about getting something of immense value? Start with feelings.

From there you can dig into more definitive components that allow you to outline your customers' experience with your brand, such as whether you want to have a very close personal relationship established with clients -- as in the case of a Realtor, or more automated as in the case of an online shopping portal.

In my coaching business, I look to establish a feeling of "safe" for my clients. So, I need to develop a more personal relationship. And although I use some form of automation to do this, it's not the primary relationship, because my face, voice and words are saddled on the automated components. Also consider if this is a one-time relationship with your client, or a long-term commitment. In my coaching business, it's about empowering entrepreneurs. So, relationship-wise, my clients get a heavy relationship investment in the short-term, and more brief relationships with touchpoints in the long-term. Similar to those perhaps of a personal trainer or a counsellor.

Finally, are you looking for a constant funnel of new, occasional, or transactional clients such as a dollar store, or a steady stream of regular clients like a hair salon? In my coaching business, I'm always looking for new clients to get started with me, and evolve on their own successfully, eventually with minimal support.

Customer Segments - This is the outright definition of your perfect client. The characteristics they carry from age, gender and relationship status or type of vehicle they drive, social activities and favourite movie of all time. You really want to understand this client. What drives them? Does the Value Proposition you developed earlier really resonate with them? How will they consume your product? Where will they most likely learn about it? Will your solution be so impactful that your clients become ambassadors for you?

Here you can build out a customer experience that works with your type of client, and again use consistent measurement and client engagement to ensure you're still their number one choice for your solution.

Keep in mind, it is totally fair to have different market segments. Especially if you have more than one key activity that might resonate with different markets. I'd suggest you focus on a primary market though and build out your idea to get a strong base first. You can always expand into future markets as you scale. Simplicity is the key to success when starting a Business Model Canvas.

Customer Channels - This is about how we reach those clients to tell them how we can solve their pain point. Channel can be more traditional methods such as TV, print and radio or digital methods such as social media, online search ads and influencer marketing. Are we using a marketing mix with multiple elements? What is the best way to connect with your client?

Channels are largely defined based on customer segments. Who your market segment is will determine how they consume media, and how you can reach them. If you told me you were using Instagram to reach an elderly demographic, I might suggest you try different channels.

Also keep in mind channels should forever be measured. Especially in the case of a marketing mix of different elements. You need to know what is working, and what isn't. What is the return on investment, and what are your clients reacting to most? Consistent tweaks to different channels can help tune your business model engine to run smoother over time.

Finally, now we can get to the nitty gritty of your idea. Let's talk about finances covered on the bottom part of the BMC.

Cost Structure - This often relates to the costs of those key activities you listed earlier (akin to direct costs on a projected revenue statement), and the costs for the business overall (general expenses). Don't get too lost in the details here. Focus more on those critical factors that you need to invest in your business for it to operate. Be realistic. This section may require a bit of research as well to ensure that it makes sense.

Revenue Streams - Again, related back to those key activities, you need to understand what you are going to charge for your product or service. Pricing here can be estimated on what your customer is willing to pay, and if your idea isn't a new one, what are they currently paying and why.

This should NOT be complicated by any means. But I'll give you the master tip my Dad (a certified professional accountant) gave me when I started in entrepreneurship:

> "Hey Bobby…Make sure your revenue exceeds your expenses." -- For real.

Why is the Business Model Canvas a good idea?

The Business Model Canvas works well because it allows you to continue to ideate and pivot your idea into a minimal viable product (or a prototype). You can try/fail many times as you work out the bugs to the idea. That's the best part. Your first "no" or first "fail" isn't the end of your idea with the BMC. It's simply a chance to pivot and try adjusting it to make it work.

It works really well within the creative economy, as every creative entrepreneur I've showcased the BMC to has had great success fleshing out the variables in their head, to produce something tangible to them…a meaningful actionable format.

It's a wonderful tool in the case of multiple ideators creating collisions in your idea. This is when you take your idea and invite someone else to add on to it. The BMC makes that process so much easier, and more organic.

It's also a quick tool to verbally vomit something out and continue to scale it over time. Note that the BMC isn't just about new ideas. Sometimes it's about adding another revenue stream to an existing business and understanding how this change affects the business overall.

Caveats

This wouldn't be a fair overview of the BMC if I didn't share some caution as well, with leveraging the BMC.

The BMC can oversimplify your idea. Although the BMC challenges you with considerations, it doesn't really propose market research to validate market readiness, but rather for you to draw from your own experience or perhaps rely on anecdotal data. Of course, using the BMC doesn't mean you can't do the research. It's just not facilitated in the nine considerations.

The BMC is best done with someone who has experience with its execution. It can be disastrous if mis-applied, taking you down rabbit holes that could give you an idea and validation based on thin air. A common misuse of the BMC is trying to use multiple variations of an idea, in one Canvas. You should consider multiple canvas' for variations/option of the same idea to ensure you can "see" all impactful variables overall.

The BMC has become popular with startups because of its quick and easy nature. But in scaleups, the BMC can again be oversimplified and is best applied over a longer period of time, with added interactions and research. In scaleup you lose the quick and easy portion for it to have more accurate impact.

More personal to me, the BMC doesn't challenge you to ask your WHY in what you do. That was a component I've personally added for my clients.

In conclusion, use it. Enjoy it. Love it. And live it. The Business Model Canvas, when applied correctly, is one of the best tools in any startup toolkit.

To learn more and make your own Business Model Canvas for your idea, visit these websites:

https://strategyzer.com/canvas/business-model-canvas

https://canvanizer.com/new/business-model-canvas

www.leanstack.com

CHAPTER 6 - FUNDING YOUR BUSINESS

Depending on your business requirements you may need startup funding to get your business off the ground. If you have a formal business plan, you may have already determined your startup costs and financial requirements for the first several years of business.

You might have enough cash in savings or investments to fund the business, especially a part-time side gig. Or you may need additional funding to properly launch and operate your business. Where do you begin?

Common sources of business financing include family and friends, banks or credit unions, investors, or government grants and loans. We will look at these options as well as relatively new financing sources like crowdfunding, below.

Family and Friends

One of the easiest sources of funding for a new business is family. You should explore this option first. Ask your parents, brothers and sisters, aunts and uncles, even grandparents if they will loan you the money to start your business. Offer to pay them back with interest.

Friends are another option to explore. They could be interested in backing your venture, or even becoming a partner. Be very careful though. If the venture fails, so might your friendship if you have not paid them back. Make sure they understand the risks before accepting financing from friends.

Banks and Credit Unions

Depending on your startup needs, a bank or credit union could be a good source of financing. Contact your bank to set up an appointment with a business loan officer. Make sure you have completed your business plan or alternative and have developed an "elevator pitch".

The elevator pitch is a 15-30 second description of your business concept, the problems it can solve and the market it will serve, and revenues it can generate.

Banks can be notoriously conservative -- and even more so for young people or new entrepreneurs. Try to come across as professional, knowledgeable and have a good handle on how much money you will need to start. Don't be afraid to share your business plan.

Make sure to visit your local credit union as well. Because credit unions are member driven, they tend to have a greater stake in their communities and may be more open to lending to individuals who don't meet all of their traditional requirements.

In Canada, the Business Development Bank of Canada, the "bank of entrepreneurs" is an arms-length agency of the federal government. The BDC has a mandate to provide funding solutions to entrepreneurs and small business, and thus is more flexible than traditional banks.

Government Funding

An often-overlooked source of startup funding is government-based or sponsored programs for small business and even specifically for young entrepreneurs.

Make sure to visit any small business assistance offices in your area to discuss potential funding (as well as any other startup assistance you may need).

In Ontario, Canada the Summer Company program offers up to $3,000 for young entrepreneurs aged 15-29, with a great idea for a summer business. Once accepted into the program, students operate their business, attend networking and training opportunities and receive mentoring over the summer. The program is delivered at Small Business Enterprise Centres across the province and has been very successful in promoting youth entrepreneurship.

Another option in Ontario is the Starter Company Plus program (age 18+) which provides up to $5,000 in funding to new and existing businesses that qualify. The program involves mandatory eight weeks of business training, and each candidate must develop and present their business plan to receive the funding.

Futurepreneur is a program for youth in Canada that provides startup funding of up to $15,000 as well as mentoring, and resources to help you start and grow your business.

The Community Futures Program is a government of Canada initiative which supports Community Futures Development Corporations throughout the country to support community economic development and small business growth.[8] These organizations offer a variety of programs including small business financing. Although interest rates may be higher than traditional banks, CFDC's can offer financing as well as business counseling and other benefits.

In the United States, the U.S. Small Business Administration provides small business loans, grants and other financial assistance programs to businesses.

Other U.S. sources of capital include the Small Business Investor Alliance which provides capital to small businesses to help them reach the next level of growth.⁹ The Small Business Lending Fund, is a U.S. Department of the Treasury program designed to help foster lending in local communities. The program is delivered through partner banks and community development loan funds throughout the United States.

There are many sources of government financing available. Visit some of the links at the end of this chapter or do an Internet search for your particular state or province to find more information.

Crowdfunding

A relatively new source of funding for business ideas is crowdfunding through services such as Kickstarter, Indiegogo and Community Funded. These platforms allow entrepreneurs to post their business ideas in order to raise the funds to create the product or service. Interested individuals pledge money towards an identified goal and if enough money is raised to fund the startup, then the project goes forward and in return funders get the product (and other bonuses), and a business is created.

An early success on Kickstarter (in 2012) was the Pebble e-paper watch. The wristwatch was designed to connect to your smartphone to alert you of calls, receive email and much more. The project was originally seeking $100,000 in startup funding but received so much publicity that it had over $10 million in advance orders within a month! The company went on to create and launch this product in 2013.[10]

Even established companies have had success with crowdfunding. In the summer of 2018, Atari (a reincarnation of the original company) launched a crowdfunding campaign on Indiegogo, to develop a new retro-gaming console named the Atari VCS. With an original goal of raising just $200,000 to finance development of the product, the company raised nearly $3 million in one day[11].

An even newer service called Upstart lets university graduates raise money from others online, to start a business, focus on their craft, writing a book or work to make a difference.[12]

Upstart provides an online environment where users create profiles with their background and goals in the hope of attracting financial backers.

Backers provide funding in exchange for a share of the graduate's future income over a 10-year period. The website determines how much money you can raise, and you choose what percentage of your income you will share.

Upstart is a new and novel way to raise funding to pursue your dreams. For more information visit www.upstart.com.

Bootstrapping Your Startup

Bootstrapping comes from the phrase "pulling yourself up by the bootstraps" and refers to the startup of a business with personal savings and subsequent use of cash-flow to grow the business. Even more on point, bootstrapping a business means building it on a budget, and relying on low-cost tactics to promote and grow the business.

Bootstrapping allows you to start a business without loans or major startup costs and grow the business without the need for outside investment. Often the founder or owner does much of the work themselves from building the website, to doing PR and social media marketing, and reinvesting any profits into growing the business.

Tactics for bootstrapping your business can include utilizing low or no-cost marketing such as social media, email marketing and word-of-mouth promotion, and avoiding significant e-commerce expenses by selling through eBay or Amazon.com, bartering with other entrepreneurs for services, and other bang-for-your-buck ideas.

I have seen many entrepreneurs forgo their own website, opting instead to build their business on Facebook and other platforms to save money. This can certainly help cut down on startup costs, as well as help to validate the business, but I would be wary of building a business on a platform that could change without notice. Facebook for example, has made changes that limit the reach of your posts to your followers.

I recommend that startups create a website early on as their home base and focus on building an email list of potential clients and customers.

Additional Resources

U.S. Small Business Administration Financial Assistance
www.sba.gov/funding-programs

Government of Canada Small Business Grants and Financing
https://canadabusiness.ca/grants-and-financing/government-grants-and-financing/

Business Crowdfunding
www.fundable.com/

Business Development Bank of Canada
www.bdc.ca

CHAPTER 7 – PREPARING TO LAUNCH

At this stage you have already developed your business idea and validated it through market research. You have written or at least started your business plan to determine how you will operate the business and show that the business is feasible. And you have determined how much money you will need to start your business.

Next, you explored the various sources of funding and financing available and have secured or made arrangements to access the startup funds for your business.

Now you are ready to move ahead and start the business. But there are still some decisions to be made.

Choosing a Business Structure

There are essentially three different business structures under which to operate the business. Each has its own set of pros and cons. These structures are listed below:

Sole Proprietorship - The business is owned by one person.

Pros
- Owner is in control
- Quick and easy to start
- Limited regulations
- Simple record keeping

Cons
- Owner is liable for all debts/obligations
- Relatively difficult to raise capital

- Lack of continuity if the owner is unable to continue the business

General Partnership - The business is owned by two or more people. The business and owners are not legally separate, and owners are jointly and separately responsible for all debts of the business.

Pros
- Two or more people can have ownership (broader management base, capital and even labor)
- Limited regulations
- Quick and easy to start
- Minimal structural / legal costs

Cons
- Owners are liable for all debts/obligations
- Potential conflict between partners
- Partnership agreement required

Incorporation - A corporation is a distinct legal entity, separate from its owner(s). Ownership is achieved through the purchase of shares in the corporation.

Pros
- Distinct legal entity
- Limited liability
- Unlimited number of owners/investors
- Easier to raise capital
- Ownership is transferrable
- Continuity

Cons
- Expensive to start
- Significant legal and accounting costs

- Closely regulated
- Extensive record keeping and administration

There are several choices to consider when starting your business. Most small businesses will register as a sole proprietor, as this is the simplest and often least expensive form of business operation.

Obviously, you would register your business as a partnership if there were multiple owners. Corporations and limited liability partnerships (in the USA) are much more complex. As stated above, due to the cost and added regulation, you would typically only consider incorporating if you require additional liability protection, the company requires significant funding, and sometimes for tax purposes.

I have personally been involved with all three types of business structures. Sole proprietorships are the easiest to operate and you make all the decisions. With a general partnership, make sure to draft a partnership agreement. You never know what will happen when two or more partners are working together. Often one partner will work more than the other, or disagreements will arise. If things go sour, the partnership agreement can help to protect your interests in the business.

Registering the Business

Depending on which business structure you choose, your next step will be to register your business with your state or provincial business authority. In the case of Ontario, Canada where I live, business registration is available online 24 hours a day at the Service Ontario website.

It is advisable to do a name search prior to registering the business, especially when incorporating (most often this is required). You don't want to find out afterwards that a business with the same name is operating in your area. This will lead to confusion and possibly legal trouble if the other business was registered first. Also, corporate names are in many cases trademarked.

Incorporation can also be done online for less than $1,000 dollars. Although, in most cases you may still require a lawyer to perform other duties such as holding and recording changes to the company's minute book and filing other paperwork on your behalf. The legal costs for any corporation can quickly become significant to the bottom line of your business!

You can file for incorporation of your business directly through your lawyer, or you can do it online. For a listing of State agencies requiring business registration, visit the U.S. Small Business Authority website: www.sba.gov/content/incorporating-your-business.

For more information on registering your business in Canada and links to provincial business registration visit: www.canadabusiness.ca/government/registering-your-business/.

Canadian Provincial, Federal and Payroll Tax

If you open your business in Canada, you may be required to register the business to collect both provincial sales tax (PST) and federal GST (goods and services tax) depending on which province you reside. If your province (eg. Ontario) has combined both taxes into one HST (harmonized sales tax), then you only need to register for an HST number. For more information, visit the following link:

www.canadabusiness.ca/government/taxes-gst-hst/provincial-and-territorial-tax-information/

You must register for GST/HST with the Canada Revenue Agency (CRA) when your total worldwide taxable income exceeds $30,000 per year, or you can register voluntarily.

You may decide to voluntarily register to collect GST/HST if you want to claim input tax credits, you expect your worldwide revenues to exceed $30,000 or your clients only do business with companies registered for GST/HST.[13]

For more information, visit the following link for a guide to Charging and Collecting Sales Tax in Canada. It is also a good idea to consult with your accountant for professional advice.

If you intend to hire employees for your business, then you are required to register for a Business Number with the Canada Revenue Agency. You can register for your Business Number, GST/HST, Payroll and Import/Export online through Canada Revenue Agency's Business registration Online website.

U.S. State, Federal and Payroll Tax

All businesses in the U.S. are required to pay federal and state taxes. Businesses must register for an Employer Identification number (EIN) with the U.S. Internal Revenue Service, as well as obtaining tax IDs and permits from your state's revenue agency.[14]

Consult with an accountant or visit the state and local tax page on the Small Business Administration's site for more details: www.sba.gov/business-guide/launch-your-business/get-federal-and-state-tax-id-numbers.

Banking, Insurance and other

Once the business is officially registered, take your paperwork to your bank or credit union and open a small business account.

There are many advantages to opening a separate business banking account. First, you will be able to receive cheques and deposit them in the business name.

You will also be able to write cheques in the business' name to pay for supplies, pay employees and all other expenses of the business. Having a separate account provides a clean paper trail for the operations of the business. This will help when doing the bookkeeping and at tax time.

And speaking of bookkeeping, it is important for you to set up an accounting system for your business. There are software packages available which allow for simplified bookkeeping -- such as Intuit Quickbooks or Sage One. You can also go the online route by trying Freshbooks or Wave. Consult with a local bookkeeper or accountant before making your decision.

Does your business require insurance to protect you or your employees against injury or against lawsuits? Depending on what kind of business you operate, you may require liability insurance or workers' compensation insurance through the government. Check with local and state/provincial regulations or consult with a local insurance representative for more details.

In Canada, there are some options geared directly to small business, like TruShield Insurance, which has pre-built insurance packages for specific types of small businesses, with the ability to add additional coverage.

Also depending on the type of business you will operate, there may be other local permits or licenses required. Check with your local municipality for such requirements. Examples would include restaurants, taxi services, food trucks and more.

Startup

Now that you have a business bank account, cheques and perhaps even a company credit card, it is time to start purchasing supplies, equipment, inventory and whatever else you may need to begin operations.

Depending on the business you have chosen, you may need office space, computer equipment, telephone service and more. A web design business for example, would require computer equipment, a printer, software, a digital camera and perhaps video equipment. You would require a desk to work at, space for storage, and perhaps even a few web design or programming books.

If you completed the startup cost exercise in chapter 4, then you already know exactly what you need to startup.

You may decide to operate the business out of your home or even out of your dorm room. These are decisions you will have made as you developed your business plan. Now it is time to implement these decisions and plans.

> *"The longer you're not taking action the more money you're losing".* – Carrie Wilkerson

For more information on registering your small business, check out the following links:

Ontario Business Registration
www.ontario.ca/page/register-business-name-limited-partnership

Small business: advice, support services, regulations
www.ontario.ca/page/small-business-advice-support-services-regulations

Canada Business Network
www.canada.ca/en/services/business.html

America's Small Business Development Centers
https://americassbdc.org/

U.S. Small Business Administration
www.sba.gov/business-guide/

You can use this handy Business Startup Checklist as you progress through the steps necessary to start your own business.

Business Startup Checklist

- ☐ Find a business idea
- ☐ Evaluate potential products or services
- ☐ Locate suppliers
- ☐ Determine pricing of products or services
- ☐ Determine target market and perform market research
- ☐ Choose a business name
- ☐ Decide on business structure
- ☐ Determine startup costs and funding needs
- ☐ Write business plan or alternative
- ☐ Register business and obtain license and permits
- ☐ Develop marketing plan
- ☐ Open business checking account
- ☐ Hire bookkeeper or accountant and setup books
- ☐ Get business insurance
- ☐ Purchase startup supplies and equipment
- ☐ Develop website and social media accounts
- ☐ Business launch

CHAPTER 8 - GETTING YOUR BUSINESS ONLINE

Having an online presence is essential for any business today. Whether you plan to sell your products or services online or not, you still need a website and an active role on social media.

Customers simply expect it.

You need a website so that customers can find you and connect with you. One of the first things people do today when looking for a business is to "Google" it or use another search engine to find information. Fewer people are using telephone books or the yellow pages to find businesses, so make sure people can find your business online. Make sure to provide your website, phone number or email address where they can reach you.

Websites are essential because they tell your story. What makes you different from other businesses in the same sector? Are you more qualified or experienced? Are your prices lower or do you carry unique products?

It is important to describe what the company offers, how the company is different, and how customers can contact you. You may even wish to sell products directly on your website.

Websites have advanced dramatically since the early days of the Internet. And the good news is web development tools have advanced as well. Gone are the days when you would have to pay a lot of money to have your website developed or rely on your 12-year-old nephew to design your site.

Depending on the scale of your website, e-commerce and security requirements etc. you may still need to hire a web design firm to build your website. But for most entrepreneurs, utilizing online tools such as www.wix.com, www.weebly.com or www.squarespace.com to design your own site is easy and affordable. This also allows you to get up and running quickly and give the business a test run without investing heavily in a website up front.

I did this myself for my most recent startup, BrandMe.Social. You can read the complete case study in Chapter 13, but essentially, I built my website in just a few hours using Wix.com and for less than $150 for the year. The service has several website templates available that you simply choose and modify. The whole process is simple, using "drag and drop" tools to add or delete components like images, plugins and other elements.

BrandMe.Social created and hosted using Wix.com

Choosing a Domain Name or URL

Once you have decided on a name for your business, one of your first steps should be to secure a website domain name. What you will find is that a lot of the best domain names are already taken. You want to find a domain that is either your business name (preferable) or describes what you have to offer.

When I launched the Adventures in Computing Camps, I bought three different domain names: www.computercamps.ca, www.computercamp.ca and www.adventuresincomputing.com. In my case, it was more important to promote what we offered than about the business itself. I ended up using the first domain as our website URL, and if anyone went to the others they were automatically redirected to the main site.

Since I had plans to expand the computer camps program to other cities in Ontario, using www.computercamps.ca to promote them made more sense than promoting my company. The name also helped with search engine rankings, and if people typed it in directly looking for information about computer camps. So, when choosing a domain name keep these things in mind.

When you are choosing a domain name I always advise that you sign up for other online services and social media platforms at the same time -- so you can reserve your name there too. I would recommend signing up on Facebook, Twitter, Instagram and other platforms even if you don't plan to use them right away.

Facebook and Other Platforms

I highly recommend having a Facebook page for your business, in addition to a website. With over 2 billion users, Facebook remains the king of social media and provides so many opportunities to share information and events with your clients, customers or fans.

By creating a Facebook page, you can share information about the business, contact information, pictures, videos and much more. See Chapter 11 for step-by-step instructions for creating your page, and tips for getting the most out of Facebook.

Because of its social nature, posting on Facebook gives you the ability to show up on the news feed of your followers, where they can like, comment or share your message. Each post has the potential to "go viral" and reach a huge audience. On the other hand, Facebook now limits the number of followers who see your messages, unless you pay to boost posts or use other techniques discussed in later chapters.

What I love about Facebook for business is the ability to reach and engage with followers for free. I rely on Facebook to promote events for my businesses and StartUP Sault Ste. Marie. Utilizing Facebook Events allows you to post an event with pictures and details, and then share the event. You can directly invite your friends and contacts, and when someone indicates that they will attend or are interested in the event, this is posted to their own timeline where their friends and family will see.

So again, it is the viral nature of Facebook that is so powerful, and because there is no cost to using the platform it is really a no-brainer.

E-commerce

E-commerce continues to grow each year as more and more people buy online. In 2017, U.S. retail e-commerce sales exceeded $450 billion, growing from $390 billion in 2016, and representing 13% of total retail sales[15].

If you intend to sell online, there are multiple platforms available for e-commerce. These range from eBay and Amazon.com to platforms like Shopify and WordPress.

The options continue to grow, while costs for the most part continue to decline. I often recommend that new entrepreneurs "try out" e-commerce for little cost or risk using eBay or Amazon.com to get their feet wet. If your products sell well on these platforms you can either stay or build e-commerce into your own website -- which ever makes the most sense.

Various e-commerce plugins are available for WordPress for example, that you can integrate into your site with a couple of clicks, allowing you to accept PayPal or credit cards right on your website.

Additional Resources

Online Sales
www.ebay.com

www.yahoosmallbusiness.com/

Amazon Services - FBA
https://services.amazon.com/fulfillment-by-amazon/benefits.html

Payment Merchants
www.paypal.com

www.moneris.com

www.squareup.com

Domains and Hosting
www.rebel.ca

www.godaddy.com

www.hostgator.com

E-commerce
www.shopify.com

www.bigcommerce.com

CHAPTER 9 – THE LAUNCH

Congratulations! You have gotten further than most. You are ready to launch your business.

Launching a business can be similar to launching any new initiative, event or program. It takes research, planning and promotion.

A good analogy is an author launching a new book. It starts with building anticipation through pre-launch marketing activities. You want to communicate with your audience about the book you are working on. And when I say audience I am referring to your following on social media, your email list and your blog.

As you are gearing up for your business launch, keep your audience informed. Engage them in the process. Need some advice on choosing a book cover? Need some help choosing your new logo? Ask your audience to vote on it.

Chris Guillebeau, the author of "The $100 Startup", "Born for This" and "Side Hustle" is a great example of an author that reaches out to his audience to get their input and their own stories. All his books use real examples and case studies to back up the information. Chris regularly engages with his audience of followers, travels the world and talks to people to find out how they have achieved success.

Book launches involve months of planning. They involve public relations to promote the upcoming launch and arrange interviews with different media. They might involve promotions on Facebook and Twitter, and video clips of the author introducing the book.

A book launch might involve building a "landing-page" website to promote the book, explain what readers will learn and direct them to where they can buy it. Contests, "bonus" deals or giveaways are often used to entice you to pre-order the book.

When an author launches a new book, they want as many people as possible to buy immediately in an attempt to be #1 in their category on Amazon or even hit the New York Times Best Seller list. The better the sales, the more your book gets promoted by others.

Entrepreneurs should think like an author or at least the publisher's marketing team.

You wouldn't open a new restaurant without getting the community excited about it, would you? Would you simply open your doors one day and hope people walking by noticed? Or would you have signs outside saying "opening soon" and advertisements announcing the opening date?

The name of the game with any business launch is to build anticipation and convert some of that interest into sales.

Whether you are launching a retail business, restaurant, online business, software, an ebook or whatever the case may be, the product launch will be different. But in every case, there are elements that will be the same.

Every new business launch should involve some or all of the following elements:

Planning. Business launches only happen once. They should be planned out thoroughly, not done on the fly. Anyone who has ever planned an event knows there are a lot of variables to consider. Choosing the right date, location, guest speakers, food and refreshments, promoting the event and getting customers to show up.

I have planned more than 50 StartUP Sault events over the last four years, including pitch nights, startup drinks, and even a major awards ceremony. Some events involve much more than others, but they all involve a plan.

Choosing the date for your event or business launch, involves more than circling a number on the calendar. First, you need to be certain that your business will be ready to open on that date. You should also consider what else is happening that day, or that week – you don't want to compete with other events that could attract your target market.

If you are opening a retail shop or restaurant, then obviously you will be hosting the launch at your shop. But what if you are launching an online business or a home-based business?

Not all launches have to involve a physical launch party. Your goal is simply to announce the new business and ensure that customers or clients will check it out and even purchase something on launch day.

Public Relations. This is an important element of the launch strategy. As mentioned earlier you want to build anticipation by staying engaged with your audience and promoting the upcoming launch. One way to do this is using a press release.

Press releases are a tool I use regularly, whether I am promoting an event, a new book, or a project I am involved in. Press releases are free to put out (you can use paid services) and all that is involved is to write it up and send it out to media sources such as the local newspaper, online news website, TV and radio stations. If you've never written a press release before, just use Google to find some examples.

Once it is sent out (typically via email), then just sit back and wait for the news media to reprint or use your release as the basis for a news story. Actually, don't sit back and wait, you have plenty of work to do! In many cases the media will contact you for comments, more detail and even full-blown interviews. Business launches are good news stories in a community, so don't underestimate how powerful a press release can be.

If your business launch is online as opposed to local, then you may wish to reach out to online news sites in your niche or use a paid service such as PR Newswire to broadcast the launch to a national or international audience. But it is the same objective – to get customers to check out your business.

Social Media. Whether it is a formal marketing campaign on Facebook, or simply letting your friends and contacts know that you are opening a business, social media can be a powerful tool. In some cases, you may already have a following or an audience that you can engage with about the launch.

On the other hand, this may be your first foray into entrepreneurship and you don't have a following yet. But you still have friends and online connections (think Facebook, LinkedIn and other networks) that you can promote to. Let them know that you are opening a business. Ask them to spread the word or share your posts. Word-of-mouth is a huge opportunity for new businesses.

Learn more about leveraging social media in Chapter 11.

Advertising. Advertising your new business launch can be essential, as in the case of a new restaurant, or it may not be necessary at all. Since advertising is about reaching your target market, the decision to advertise the launch of your business will often depend on whether the business is online or has a physical location.

Launching a new business in a physical location, such as retail or a service business, typically involves a special event such as a grand opening, with special guests (perhaps the Mayor), refreshments and product specials. Local advertising can drive traffic to the store as well as making people aware that the new business exists.

Good sources for local advertising include online news websites, newspapers, radio, and Chamber of Commerce mailouts and newsletters. If you had help from your local small business resource centre or economic development agency, make sure to ask if they will help promote the launch as well. They are usually more than happy to help promote their clients as it looks good on them as well.

Launching a new online business such as an e-commerce site will involve reaching much larger audiences than a local business. Online advertising may involve Google Ads to target certain keywords, display advertisements and other online marketing tools.

Learn more about promoting your business in Chapter 10.

Grand Opening Event. The grand opening event can be a huge opportunity for a local business in a physical location. It is a way to rally friends and family for support and can often generate even more local press and recognition in the community. If you've planned well and promoted the launch you could experience a lot of foot traffic and make some sales your first day.

The event should provide an incentive for people to attend and check out the new business. It is a great way to make a good first impression. As you speak to your customers and attendees you might also get some great feedback on what they like about the store or what products they would love you to carry.

The business launch is an important event for your business. Whether it is a formal launch or simply a personal recognition that you are "open for business", it is a milestone representing the beginning of your new journey into entrepreneurship.

The launch should be acknowledged and recognized at whatever level makes sense for you and your business. Focusing on the elements discussed in this chapter will help ensure a successful launch and a great start for your new business.

CHAPTER 10 - PROMOTING YOUR BUSINESS

Marketing is one of the most important functions of running a business. There are many types of marketing and promotion available, and it is essential to figure out the best "mix" to attract customers and grow your business, while staying within your budget.

It is important to understand who your target market is before spending any money on marketing. How will you best reach potential clients or customers? Through television or radio? Through newspaper advertisements or online? Once again, while developing your business plan, you will have considered these questions.

Many of the small businesses I have worked with have small marketing budgets and are therefore looking for the biggest bang for their buck. Often this can be achieved through online marketing, social media, email marketing, word-of-mouth promotion and other creative marketing ideas.

Much of the marketing I do personally and for my businesses is done online. I have multiple websites and utilize social media extensively.

In the early 2000's when I owned Adventures in Computing Camps, I advertised in the local newspaper, but relied heavily on some cost-effective tools such as flyers (I would often print up to 15,000 for less than $500 and distribute in the elementary school system locally for free), and our email list was gold.

When parents registered their children for camp, I made sure to ask if they wanted to receive our email newsletter. Visitors could also join our email list right on the website. Since returning campers was a huge portion of our business, having the ability to send camp information to our email list was important and very effective. Word-of-mouth was also an effective marketing tool for the camps. These methods were inexpensive but extremely effective.

TIP: When running your marketing campaigns always attempt to track their effectiveness by asking customers how they heard about your business. On our camp registration form we always asked parents how they heard about the camps (by listing all of the marketing mediums we used that year). Since we utilized flyers in the schools, internet banner ads, our website, as well as newspaper advertising and others, it was important to determine what worked most effectively.

Reaching Your Target Market

In developing your marketing plan or evaluating your options, it is important to think in terms of reaching your target market, which you identified in chapter 3. Knowing who your ideal customer is will make it much easier to choose the most effective forms of advertising.

Traditional Media

Traditional media includes advertising on radio, television, newspaper, billboards and typically any other kind of mass media. These mediums allow you to reach large audiences that include potential customers and clients.

With traditional media it is possible to target segments of the population but may not be effective for all businesses -- depending on what your goals are. Mass media can be effective for brand awareness, and specific demographics can be targeted -- by choosing to advertise during a certain TV show, or placing an ad in a teen girl magazine, for example.

Any of the traditional media will provide a break-down of their demographic profile. For example, the Toronto, Canada-based Globe & Mail newspaper is a national newspaper with over 1.1 million weekday readers. According to their media kit[16], the weekday readership breaks down as follows:

Male: 58.7%
Female: 41.3%
Ages:
Under 34: 31%
35-49: 20%
50-64: 26%
65+: 23%

Millennials represent the largest group of readers of Globe & Mail with 31%, up from just 18% in 2012, when the 1st edition of this book was published. Ages 35-49 decreased from 26% to 20%, ages 50-64 decreased from 31% to 26%, and 65+ remained the same at 23%. In 2012, more than 80% of Globe & Mail readers were white collar professionals with an average household income of $101,100, and now only 38% of readers earn more than $100,000.

As we can see, it is important to check a media channel's reader demographic. In this case above, the demographic has shifted dramatically in the last 6 years and it may no longer represent a good choice to reach your customers.

When developing your marketing strategy, speak with traditional media sources in your area (or nationally) to find out the demographics of their readers or listeners and the cost of advertising with them.

Online Marketing

Online advertising grew 21% in 2017 to $88 billion, and exceeded the advertising spent on TV for the first time.[17] Mobile advertising accounted for nearly $50 billion of 57% of the total digital ad spend. As consumers spend more and more time online reading news, visiting social networks, watching videos and playing games, advertisers are moving more and more of their budgets to online media.

The choices for small business continue to grow and the ability to reach consumers within your target market are much more precise. Below are some of the different forms of online marketing available to small businesses.

Search Engine Listings

Google and other search engines are still the leading provider of traffic to Internet websites. It is important for your website to rank high for keyword searches related to your business. Instead of sifting through a phone book, many people now just search online for a business that can meet their needs.

In 2017, Google remained the leading search engine with nearly 75% of traffic, followed by Baidu with 15% and Microsoft Bing at about 8%. Yahoo and other like AOL hold just a few percentage points each.

When you design your website or have it designed, keep search engine optimization (SEO) in mind to ensure your site ranks well. Focusing on the three top search engines makes the most sense.

Google Ads

The next step in search engine marketing is to pay for your website to display prominently when someone searches for the products or services that you offer. These are called sponsored links, and perhaps the best example is Google Ads.

With Google Ads, you can set a budget to bid on certain keywords so that when someone types in "computer camp" for example, the search would return a listing of websites along with your text advertisement directing viewers to click through to your website.

Sponsored links are a popular way to drive traffic to your website. But they can be expensive – so ensure that you have a sufficient budget for an effective campaign. Visit https://ads.google.com for more details.

Online Display Advertising

Graphic ads of varying sizes are still quite popular on the web. Whether you purchase ad space on a local news site or purchase a campaign to appear on various websites in an ad network, banner advertisements may or may not be effective for your business.

The idea is for viewers to see your ad and click through to your website to find out more about the business or to purchase your products or services. Since my computer camps business was a seasonal business, when I did purchase advertising on a local high-traffic news website, I would typically purchase ads in May, June and July only. The timing would ensure that the ads were seen in the period leading up to summer camp season – when most parents are planning their vacation time.

Depending on your product or service, banner ads may not be a the most effective form of advertising. They can help to create brand awareness, however, and can be effective in local markets.

Facebook Ads

In 2012, Facebook surpassed one billion users and today there are over two billion active users. Facebook still presents a huge opportunity for marketers. With the amount of personal data Facebook has access to, their ads can target your exact audience.

Imagine typing in the details of your perfect customer. Facebook ads have this ability. You can target your ad by location, sex, age, interests, relationship status, job title, workplace, or college for example.

Your ads will only show up on the page of individuals who meet your particular requirements. When you log into Facebook and go to Ads Manager, you can enter your target market information and see how many users match your customer profile.

With Facebook ads you can choose to be charged for the number of clicks you receive (CPC) or the number of impressions of your ad that are displayed (CPM). For more details, visit www.facebook.com/marketing.

Facebook remains a powerful marketing tool for any business. While it is easy to use, results are not guaranteed. I recommend clients try out Facebook ads with a modest budget. But if you find you are spending large sums of money without a corresponding increase in sales, then consider hiring a social media marketing firm to develop a more effective campaign.

Email Marketing

Email marketing can be a powerful way to share your message and sell your products or services. I highly recommend giving visitors to your website the ability to sign up for your newsletter or simply more information. When someone signs up by providing their email address, they are "opting in" to receive valuable information from you in the future.

This gives you the ability to send emails to customers at a later time. These emails should include useful information, promotions, details of upcoming sales, product profiles or tips.

Email marketing was one of the most effective tools for promoting my computer camps. Since a large proportion of registrations (over 50%) each year were from returning campers, it was important for us to be able to keep parents up to date on our camp schedules, discounts and promotions. We actively built an email list of over 300 parents by asking for their email address on our camp registration form and directly on our website.

Through the use of online email services such as Constant Contact, MailChimp or AWeber you can not only manage your email list, but also monitor each email for effectiveness. These services will provide reports on how many and which people opened your email, what links were clicked, and even if the email was forwarded or shared via social media! Very powerful stuff.

I recommend building this capability into your website early on. Try to send only valuable information or content – don't bombard your list with hard selling or unrelated materials. Treat your list like the gold that it is.

Blogging and Other Online Activities

Although things have changed a lot since the 1st edition of this book, I still think blogging can help build your business. Blogging creates the opportunity for you to showcase your skills, knowledge and expertise in a subject. It provides a very effective method of building your personal brand.

Blogging can take many forms – including product reviews, advice, or general commentary. Most successful blogs focus on a particular niche. In your case, a blog might be a great outlet for providing advice to your customers and potential customers. The more knowledgeable and helpful you appear on your blog, the more credibility you can earn – and this can translate directly into sales.

I have been writing about business and technology for many years, both through traditional media and blogging. In 2013 the Blackberry marketing team reached out to me on LinkedIn to tell me they had been following my technology blog and liked what they were reading. I had written several blog posts about new Blackberry phones and what the company was up to.

Based on what they had seen, they invited me to join the Blackberry Elite program, which utilized a couple of hundred "influencers" around the world to promote Blackberry within their networks and through social media. I spent five years in the program, received free devices every year, and even attended the launch of their new operating system, BB10, in New York City (all expenses paid). It was a surreal experience and it all happened because I was blogging about technology and had written some positive reviews of Blackberry devices.

As your blog grows in popularity, and builds regular traffic, you may be able to sell advertising or utilize Google AdSense to show relevant ads on your site and get paid a fee for each click. This is how many bloggers make a living.

There are rules for blogging that are smart to follow, including respecting copyrighted materials such as images, and content from other websites. If you are reviewing or giving a plug to a product which you sell, you should be open and honest about this. Readers will appreciate your honesty and trust what you are saying. You don't want readers to think you are simply trying to pimp your products!

If you do intend to start blogging for your business, it would be a good idea to see what others are doing. Do some research. Are your competitors blogging? Do an Internet search for "rules for blogging" and you will find several useful articles on the subject.

Free and Low-Cost Marketing Ideas

In every business I have operated and every event I have organized, I have always utilized free and low-cost marketing tools and media.

As I mentioned previously, when promoting my computer camps, I found a way for my target audience to bring camp flyers home to their parents. I simply asked the local school boards (elementary and high school) if teachers could distribute flyers directly to the students in the appropriate grades.

Guess what? They said yes. For less than $500 I was able to print and distribute 15,000 flyers every year directly to the class rooms in my city with students aged 7-13. This was way more effective than any newspaper advertisement. Combining this low-cost technique with our growing email list of current and past parents, and our budget for marketing was remarkably low.

Some of the tools I highly recommend include leveraging social media (more on this later), using press releases to get local and sometimes national coverage, online contests/giveaways, embracing video (across mediums), and building your email list. All of these methods are low-cost yet extremely powerful in promoting your products, services and your business.

There are many more low-cost marketing ideas, ranging from the obvious to unique or different. Below are 20 more ideas:

1. Flyers/posters – pass them out or post in high traffic areas.
2. Business cards – always bring to networking events and meetings.
3. Get a banner-up – banner-ups are professional looking and can make an impact, especially at speaking gigs or tradeshows.
4. Post cards – affordable, professional looking, and great as a handout.
5. T-shirts – can be effective for giveaways, especially if you have a cool logo, slogan or design.
6. Guest speaking at events/seminars – what better way to showcase yourself as an expert?
7. Write a column for local newspaper – I continue to do this. It is great for building your personal brand.
8. Networking – is usually free and is very effective for building your network and making connections that can help your business.

9. Join groups/volunteer – don't volunteer just to build your business, but it is great side effect. We often choose to do business with people we know.
10. Write a book to build expertise and authority.
11. Print your website URL on store receipts, bags etc.
12. Word-of-mouth is a powerful way to build a business. Do a good job and treat your customers right, and they will tell their friends. But remember, the same is true if they are unhappy with your business.
13. Use free giveaways and incentives to collect emails to build your list.
14. Testimonials – always effective and are free. Social proof is very powerful, so make sure to get a few.
15. Promotional gifts with your website URL.
16. Offer referral rewards. It costs money to acquire new clients, so if your existing customers deliver them to you, make sure to give them a little something in return.
17. Chamber of Commerce flyers and email blasts – these are typically very affordable and if your target market is other businesses and entrepreneurs then even better.
18. Reward brand champions with free swag. You would be amazed at how far this can go. The amount of positive social media promotion and loyalty Blackberry got out of me (and hundreds more brand advocates) for the cost of a free smartphone, t-shirts and other swag was priceless!
19. Email signature – One of the easiest ways to promote your businesses and projects is to list your various job titles, websites and social media handles on every email you send out!
20. Develop your elevator pitch so you can tell people what you do in 15 seconds. This will pay dividends at your next networking event!

Additional Resources

Entrepreneur.com Marketing Articles
http://www.entrepreneur.com/marketing/index.html

Steps to a Google-friendly Website
https://support.google.com/webmasters/answer/40349?hl=en&ref_topic=3309300

10 Small Business Marketing Tips: 2018 Edition
www.primoprint.com/blog/10-small-business-marketing-tips-2018-edition/

CHAPTER 11 - LEVERAGING SOCIAL MEDIA

> *"Social media gives entrepreneurs and businesses an unprecedented chance to engage with their customers and communicate their message."* [Gary Vaynerchuk – Crush it!]

Back in 2012, in the 1st edition of this book, social media marketing had its own chapter because it was still relatively shiny and new. In this revised and updated 2nd edition, social media marketing still has its own chapter – because it is so effective.

Social media is indispensable for today's businesses. From its influence, and ability to reach massive audiences, customers and friends, social media should be an important part of any business' marketing efforts.

Social media gives you the power to connect, communicate and most importantly listen to your customers, competitors and brand champions.

We all use it but what is social Media?

Defining social media can be a challenge. A quick search on the Internet will bring up hundreds of references and definitions, but most don't get to the heart of what it really is. It is a change in how we communicate, share information, and converse with others. Two solid definitions in my opinion include:

> *"Social media essentially is a category of online media where people are talking, participating, sharing, networking, and bookmarking online."*
> (Ron Jones, Search Engine Watch)

and

> *Social media are computer-mediated technologies that facilitate the creation and sharing of information, ideas, career interests and other forms of expression via virtual communities and networks.* (Wikipedia)

There are numerous examples of social media, including social networks (Facebook, LinkedIn), blogs, micro-blogging (Twitter), content communities (YouTube, Instagram, Pinterest), forums and more. You probably already use most of these on a personal level.

According to the 2018 Social Media Marketing Industry Report, the top five social media networks/tools for marketers are: Facebook, Instagram, Twitter, LinkedIn, and YouTube, in that order.[18] In other words, these are the platforms most used by professional marketers to promote their company's products, services or brands.

If you used the top five you would be off to a good start, but there are others, like Pinterest or Snap Chat, that can provide additional opportunities for your business.

Using social media to help promote your business may seem obvious to many of you, but when I speak to business owners (of all ages) about social media, it really helps to answer the question "why should I use social media" by putting things in perspective with statistics on social media use:

- There were 2.46 billion social network users in 2017 – nearly 71% internet users (eMarketer).
- 81% of consumers' purchasing decisions are influenced by their friends' social media posts (Forbes).

- Over 5 billion videos are watched on YouTube every day, and 300 hours of video are uploaded every minute (Merchdope).
- According to Facebook, 100 million hours of video content is viewed on its platform every day.
- 70% of social media usage occurs on mobile devices (Marketing Land).
- Users spend an average of 135 minutes on social media per day (Statista).
- In 2017, 88% of Millennials used Facebook (Sprout Social).

We will look at some of the most popular options below and I highly recommend you spend time investigating the different social media platforms to decide which tools will work best for you and your business. Then use them regularly for marketing, customer service, market research, and connecting with your customers.

Top Social Media Platforms

Facebook is the top social networking site with over two billion users worldwide. You can set up a company page for free and when people "Like" your page, they subscribe to receive updates in their news feed. Additionally, if your followers comment on or like your posts, it will show up in their newsfeed as well -- setting you up for even greater exposure.

Facebook has built in some great analytical tools to measure the social reach of your page, and all of your posts -- including how many people have seen your post, clicked on it, and how many have interacted with the post by commenting, "liking" or sharing the post.

This information really helps you to determine which posts, messages and even images that you are sharing is connecting with others on Facebook.

It should be noted that Facebook has implemented changes to their algorithm that now limit the organic or natural reach of posts. In other words, posts are becoming less effective for reaching followers, resulting in the need to spend more money on Facebook ads and "boosted" posts.

Below are some tips and suggestions for using Facebook for your business:

1. Sign up with Facebook to create your company page. Simply login and select "create page" on the bottom left of the screen. From there select "Business or Brand", or "Community or Public Figure", depending on your business.
2. Obtain a Facebook URL so people can find your business easily (www.facebook.com/yourbusiness).
3. Add relevant information to your Facebook page including a description of your business, products and services offered, your specialties, hours of operation etc.
4. Make sure to include your business address and contact information such as phone number, email address and a link to your website.
5. Post updates to your wall including business activities, promotions and incentives.
6. Post links to articles, research data or share other relevant and engaging content that would be of interest to your followers.

7. Post upcoming events you are hosting as well as any tradeshows, conferences and other programs where you or someone from your company will be present.
8. Hold Facebook contests or promotions to encourage people to "like" and engage with your page (ensure to follow Facebook terms of use).
9. Consider utilizing Facebook ads to target and grow your audience (give it a try with a $10 budget for starters).
10. Post new content, offers and promotions regularly. A good rule to follow is the 80/20 rule in terms of how often you should push or promote the businesses products or services to your audience. Therefore 80% of content should be helpful and engaging, with just 20% or less actually promoting your business.

Instagram is a photo and video-sharing social network owned by Facebook. The platform boasts over 800 million users and continues to grow rapidly.

Instagram allows you to follow other users and creates a "newsfeed" of images and video clips. You can also search for photos by subject or hashtag.

In 2018, Instagram introduced Instagram Stories allowing photo and video sequences that disappear in 24 hours. This allows users to have some fun and get creative, while telling a story and providing value.

Brands are using Instagram to sell products, promote fashion, provide tutorials for their users and much more. Millennials are the largest demographic on Instagram.

As an added bonus, images posted to Instagram can automatically post on Facebook as well.

A great introduction to Instagram can be found here: https://blog.hootsuite.com/how-to-use-instagram-for-business/

Twitter is a micro-blogging site (280-character messages or "tweets"), used to share content and follow knowledgeable and influential people in your fields of interest. Twitter can be a powerful tool for sharing information, and news. Once a large follower base is built, it can also be an excellent tool for promoting your business.

I was not a huge proponent of Twitter in the beginning. I suppose I didn't fully grasp the potential, especially for business. While encouraging me to start using Twitter back in 2010, a friend simply explained that *"Facebook is for people you know. Twitter is for people you want to know."* In other words, we use Facebook (personal page) to communicate and share with friends, family and others that we know personally. Twitter is more about discovering and following people we'd like to know, learn from or do business with. It made sense.

Twitter allows you to learn from and communicate with people of interest, experts, customers, and others in real-time. In many cases, Twitter represents the pulse of what is happening around the world.

By looking at what is "trending" you can see the most popular terms on Twitter, in real-time.

Below are some tips and suggestions for using Twitter for your business:

1. Although your Twitter following will build organically over time, this can be accelerated by following individuals and businesses in your community.

2. Start by building a base and then following individuals and companies that are relevant to your products or services. Remember, those you follow will also be providing tweets that you can in turn share.

3. Share company news, and interesting or relevant content.

4. Twitter for businesses is more than talking about "what are you doing". Focus more on creating or providing value to your followers or demonstrating your expertise.

5. When promoting a blog post or article on your website, explain why clicking the link will provide followers something of value.

6. Use Twitter Search and monitor your notifications for "mentions" of your account, to see what people are saying about your business, products or services. Try to participate in the conversation where it makes sense.

7. Commenting on others' tweets, and retweeting what others have posted is a great way to build community and add new followers.

8. Promote sales or special promotions, but again, stick to the 80/20 rule – no more than 20% of tweets should be self-promotion.

9. Twitter is a communication platform that will help you interact with potential and existing customers.

10. Build your brand and your followers by being helpful and sharing useful information. Don't be afraid to tag others as well to spur conversation and increase your reach.

As Gary Vaynerchuk says, *"when someone re-tweets what you say, they're saying you're smart and worth paying attention to. That comes with a lot of value." (Crush it!)*

NOTE: Building a Twitter following takes time and effort, but there is a payoff. The value of Twitter for your business increases as you add more and more followers.

A simple strategy for building a solid Twitter following is to begin by following experts, leaders and others of interest. In my case I focused on authors, entrepreneurs and thought leaders. I began to tweet relevant information as well as retweeting valuable information from those that I followed. As soon as I became active on Twitter, others began to follow me and retweet my posts as well. This is how you build momentum and gain followers.

LinkedIn is a professional social networking site which can be used to promote yourself, build your personal brand, make contacts and potentially gain business. There are over 500 million users on LinkedIn.

LinkedIn is not just a professional resume site. It provides opportunities to meet or target other business owners, executives, and professionals from around the world. One of LinkedIn's greatest strengths is the ability to search for potential clients and customers by company or even job title.

LinkedIn in my opinion is the number one platform for building a professional personal brand. The site has been evolving somewhat as more and more users share meaningful content and their own stories.

Thought leaders abound on LinkedIn, everyone from Gary Vaynerchuk, Ryan Holmes (CEO of Hootsuite), and Mark Schaefer are regular contributors with top content and insights. It is also possible to grow your brand and become an influencer yourself on LinkedIn as demonstrated by Michaela Alexis, Manu Goswami and Josh Fechter.

YouTube is the largest video website (over 1.5 billion users) on the Internet and provides an opportunity to promote your brand and showcase your expertise through the creation and sharing of short videos.

Similar to blogging, YouTube and other video sites provide the ability to connect with consumers, clients and customers in a personal manner. Ideas include product reviews and demonstrations, funny or entertaining videos to create goodwill and even tutorials. Again, by offering free information you are adding value while presenting yourself as knowledgeable on the topic.

YouTube can provide significant advantages to your business because of its huge user base, the ability for users to search for videos based on relevant keywords, and perhaps the biggest bonus, the ease of which viewers can share videos! Consider the power of sharing when you come across the next viral video on your Facebook page or even on the news. Viral videos can rack up millions of views in a matter of hours...what would this do for your business?

Pinterest is a platform that allows their 175 million users to organize and "pin" images, videos and other visual content. The examples are endless, but think about all of the decorating ideas, wedding ideas, clothing styles, recipes, diagrams and other images you find everyday while surfing.

Pinterest lets you organize and share images you find on the Internet. You can categorize and pin them on different "boards", so that you can check them out again later, and others can see them as well. Every image you and others pin is linked back to the original source -- which could be your website.

You may be asking how this can help your business. If you sell products or deliver services which can be reflected well visually through images, Pinterest could be an ideal social network to drive traffic to your website or sell directly on Pinterest using the "buy button."

Imagine if you operated an interior decorating business, a bakery or built custom decks for homes in your community. What if you were an author and posted images of all your book covers? All of these businesses and professions could benefit greatly from posting pictures of their finished products on Pinterest and linking back to their website.

Other users can and will repin your pictures to their own boards, "like" or even comment on them, helping your pictures (and your business) to gain even more exposure. If you haven't used Pinterest before, it is definitely worthwhile to check it out at www.pinterest.com.

A Few Tips

- Spend some time investigating the different social media platforms.

- Decide which tools will work best for you and your business, then start using them.

- Promote your use of social media on your website, business cards, email signature etc.

- Use Facebook, Instagram and Twitter to build your brand – whether that brand is your business or YOU!

- Keep your eyes open for new and better tools available, social media is constantly evolving.

Additional Resources

Mashable – Social Media Marketing
http://mashable.com/follow/topics/social-media-marketing/

Top Social Media Management Tools
https://www.entrepreneur.com/article/290732

7 Steps in Creating a Winning Social Media Marketing
https://sproutsocial.com/insights/social-media-marketing-strategy/

How to Create a Social Media Marketing Strategy in 8 Steps
https://blog.hootsuite.com/how-to-create-a-social-media-marketing-plan/

CHAPTER 12 - I'M IN BUSINESS, NOW WHAT?

Some might say the hard part is over but running your business won't always be a walk in the park. You are going to experience highs and lows, challenges, great experiences and maybe some not-so-great experiences. Don't ever give up or get discouraged.

To reap success, you will need to work hard. But the lessons learned, and confidence gained will make it all worthwhile. Below is some further guidance to consider as you operate and grow your business:

Enjoy it. Enjoy being the owner of your own business, and the many perks it might provide. Depending on the kind of business you operate, you may be able to make your own hours, or have the flexibility to work less. Enjoy the feeling of accomplishment and satisfaction you will get from starting and growing your own business.

Stay on top of things. Even very successful businesses can be improved. Now that you are in business, you should track your progress. Track the success of your marketing, monitor cash-flow and the finances of the business. Make improvements. If something isn't working, fix it or change things to make it work better. Continually tweaking operations to be more efficient, effective and more profitable can make the difference between running a good business and running a great business!

Don't be short sighted. When running a business, it is beneficial to operate in terms of long-term success, rather than making quick cash or quick benefits. Investing in the business to make it more efficient over the long-term can result in significantly more profits down the road, as opposed to saving a few dollars now.

"Successful people are always looking for opportunities to help others. Unsuccessful people are asking, What's in it for me?" – Brian Tracy

Focus on the customer. Customer service should take high priority for both you and your staff. We've all heard the saying, "The customer is always right." Is it true? Of course not, but we need to do everything in our power to make the customer's experience with our business a good one. This might include offering a fair return policy or offering a discount if the order was screwed up.

Our second year in business we made the decision to cancel a particular computer camp due to low enrolment. I was personally calling customers to let them know and to explain the process of getting a refund. One customer was very disappointed, because their son had been looking forward to learning to make video games at our camp for months. In fact, the family lived in Toronto, Ontario and had made plans to take a family vacation in Sault Ste. Marie (an 8-hour drive) while their son attended camp.

Even though I could have said I was sorry and hoped they may book again the next year, I not only apologized, but offered to send a camp T-shirt and a free copy of the software program we used in the course! The customer was thrilled. The next year, not only did her son attend camp, but he brought a friend!

Customers are a business' lifeblood. Do everything you can to ensure they return the next time. It is much easier and less expensive to keep an existing customer than it is to get a new one. Make sure they are a priority.

Listen to your customers. Your customers have an amazing ability to see what can be improved in your business. Listen to them. Request feedback after the sale and ask your customers to connect with you on social media and other platforms (surveys, how was our service cards, etc.). Don't wait until that feedback becomes negative online comments or word-of-mouth.

> *"Your most unhappy customers are your greatest source of learning."* – Bill Gates

Monitor social media for any comments or discussions about your business. If the discussion is negative, apologize for the bad experience and attempt to rectify the situation. Take the discussion offline either through direct message, email or telephone. By making the situation right, you can avoid these potentially damaging comments from being viewed. Do the right thing.

Always look for new business. Now that your business is off the ground and you are experiencing success, don't rest on your laurels. Focus on building the business by acquiring new clients or customers. Think strategically when it comes to growth, embrace new opportunities, seek out new products and services your business can provide, and be open to working with other businesses to drive continued growth.

Keep these tips in mind as you operate, and you will grow your business, gain customers, and limit bad reviews or perceptions.

CHAPTER 13 – SIDE HUSTLE CASE STUDY

For most wantrepreneurs (wannabe entrepreneurs), coming up with the right business idea is often the biggest obstacle. But sometimes an opportunity falls in your lap that you didn't consider before. I consider myself a serial entrepreneur, having started many different businesses over the years, and this recently happened to me.

As an entrepreneur, I am always thinking about different business ideas and opportunities. I have operated various types of businesses over the years (nearly all part-time), everything from web design, computer camps, consulting, training, blogging, indie book publishing, online product sales and more. But a recent experience spurred my latest side business or "side hustle" if you will.

A friend reached out to me, asking if I could help his colleague with their resume. Over the last decade or so I had helped numerous friends and family members to build or revamp their resumes, with great success. Since my free time was at a premium, I agreed to help for $50 per hour and they accepted.

First, I reviewed the client's existing resume and then we met for coffee to get into more detail about her work history, skills and ambitions for the future. I really enjoyed the process. The result was a much more powerful resume, and my client was very pleased.

Then it occurred to me. Everyone I had helped over the years had experienced success with their new resumes…they had either gotten the job they were after or at the very least landed interviews. They also felt much more confident with their qualifications.

It turned out I had a knack for helping people extract valuable transferable skills and accomplishments from their work history, including many they didn't even realize they had. Through my own experience and background, I had learned which skills and talents make someone a valuable team member. I could then wordsmith these accomplishments, crafting a narrative in the form of an attractive, powerful resume.

And now I realized clients were willing to pay me for this service.

I am not a certified resume writer, or job counselor…so what qualifies me to help clients with their resume? It turns out that my nearly 20 years of experience in business development, marketing, entrepreneurship, management, and personal branding has given me an edge. I had hired my own employees and had been involved in hiring at several positions I had held over the years. I knew what skills I looked for in candidates and had worked with enough talented colleagues to recognize the skills necessary to be successful and effective in any organization.

Shortly after my own revelation, I began the process of establishing and launching my new service. It would focus on resume development and personal brand development – something I had success with, as a published author, brand advocate for Blackberry, and Startup Canada Award winner. With hard work and a plan, it is possible to craft your own story, while building authority and expertise in a particular niche or industry.

How does this apply to you? Think about it. We all have talents, experience and qualifications that we can utilize to operate a side hustle. Would you be happy making extra money in your spare time doing something you enjoy?

Side hustles are often low-cost operations that fit your schedule, and your lifestyle. Work as much or as little as you'd like (in your spare time), and who knows, you might find there is enough demand (and satisfaction) to someday make it a full-time venture.

With this in mind, I will describe each step and the costs incurred to launch my new business in less than a week. It is easier and less expensive than you might think!

1. Choose a business name. Sometimes it helps to see if the website domain name is available. I had several ideas, but I liked BrandMe.Social best, because I felt it effectively described the service I offered, and the .social (top level domain) is relatively new and unique. Cost = $20

2. Register your business. It is important to register the business with your province or state to make it official. In my case the Ontario government charges $60 for a sole proprietor or partnership. Incorporation costs significantly more. Cost = $60

3. Get a logo and branding. Having a visual and easily identifiable logo is important for brand recognition. Branding takes the colors and style of your logo and extends it to things like social media banners, letterhead, business cards etc. It is a good idea to maintain a common appearance and theme. Cost = $45 (using www.fiverr.com – a website where freelancers from around the world offer various services, often starting at $5).

4. Having a website is essential for businesses today. While some small businesses utilize a Facebook Page as their online presence (which certainly is a good idea), having a dedicated website in my opinion is still a necessity. Facebook is great for connecting with customers socially, but a website can have more content, more capabilities and align better with your

brand. I opted to build a website using www.wix.com which had several templates to choose from and included one year of hosting. Check it out at www.brandme.social . Cost = $140

5. Networking is essential for building a business, so my last purchase was business cards. I utilized www.vistaprint.ca and found a design that went well with my website and branding. I customized the text myself and uploaded my logo. I received 250 cards in the mail in less than a week! Cost = $20

6. Promotion. Tell your friends and family about your new venture. Ask for referrals. Share on social media and start engaging with potential clients. Get the word out using free techniques before spending any money on advertising and promotion. Cost = FREE

You might have noticed that the grand total was actually $285. However, in my case I did not register the new business, as I intend to offer the service under another existing business I operate, saving me $60. Therefore, I only spent $225.

It is important to recognize that there are some other important steps along the way. As soon as I decided on the business name/domain name, I made sure to secure the name on Facebook, Twitter, YouTube, and other social media platforms. Again, you want to be consistent across mediums so that your customers and clients can find you.

You may have also noticed that I did not mention writing a business plan and performing a lot of market research to ensure the business was feasible. I did make a plan, but it was a one-page business plan – identifying what my ideal client looks like, our unique selling proposition (what makes us different), how I will market the service, a startup budget and more.

Since this is another side business for me, there isn't a lot of risk. There is no inventory or major expenses to incur. Because I am offering a service, it is just my time, which is valuable to me, but doesn't technically cost me anything.

Because my costs are so low, this is a worthwhile venture even with one client a month.

Once my website was complete, I shared the news of this new service on Facebook and LinkedIn. My Facebook page already has over 40 likes and continued to grow. From there I was confident I could connect with new clients through word-of-mouth referrals and social media alone. To date, I have not spent any money on advertising, but instead rely on social media and word-of-mouth.

Feel free to check out my website at www.brandme.social. I'd love to hear your feedback or answer any questions you may have about starting your own side business.

The easiest way to get into business is to get started with as little cost and risk as possible. I have shown you how to launch a new business in a week for less than $250. What is holding you back?

146

RECOMMENDED RESOURCES

There are so many valuable online resources available for new entrepreneurs. Below are additional resources that will aid in your success. I encourage you to check them out now, or use the as a reference as you go through the business startup process:

Business Ideas:
www.startupbizhub.com/ - a business ideas blog

www.entrepreneur.com/businessideas - Business Idea Center

General Business Resources:
www.blogtrepreneur.com - a small business blog with lots of content and tools for entrepreneurs and small business.

www.marsdd.com/entrepreneurs-toolkit/ - an excellent toolkit of business resources, workbooks, funding source directory and more. From MaRS, where science, technology and social entrepreneurs get the help they need.

www.mikemichalowicz.com/resources/ - free business resources, downloads and articles.

Canadian Business Resources:
www.canadabusiness.ca/eng/ - Canada Business Network. Provides information and resources for starting a business anywhere in Canada.

www.bizpal.ca - a website service which streamlines the business permit and licensing experience throughout Canada.

www.cfib-fcei.ca/en - Canadian Federation of Independent Business (CFIB)

http://www.ic.gc.ca/eic/site/ic1.nsf/eng/h_00006.html - Industry Canada business website (including patents and intellectual property)

http://www.investcanada.ca/ - Invest Canada website. Provides industry research, business resources and government publications, including sector reports.

www.ontario.ca/page/business-and-economy - government resources and information for starting and operating a business in Ontario, Canada.

Financing:
www.cbo-eco.ca/en/index.cfm/financing/government-loans-and-grants/financing-a-business-guide/ - Financing a Business Guide (Canada)

https://nohfc.ca/en/ - Northern Heritage Funding programs for Northern Ontario businesses.

https://www.thoughtco.com/money-to-start-a-small-business-3321753 - U.S. Government money for small business

http://www.sba.gov/category/navigation-structure/loans-grants/small-business-loans - SBA Small Business Loans

Market Research:
www.census.gov - United States Census

www.statcan.gc.ca - Statistics Canada demographics and information

Mentoring:
http://www.score.org/ - free business mentoring in the U.S.

U.S. Business Resources:
www.sba.gov/ - the U.S. Small Business Administration

www.usa.gov/business - a business portal for businesses startup, growth, exporting and other opportunities for U.S. companies.

Young Entrepreneurs:
https://www.entrepreneur.com/topic/young-entrepreneurs - a small business blog focusing on youth entrepreneurship.

http://bizkids.com/business-resources - BizKids TV show

ABOUT THE AUTHOR

Nevin M. Buconjic is an award-winning serial entrepreneur, author, strategic advisor and community builder. Nevin holds degrees in marketing, computer science and an MBA, and has over 20 years of experience in business, finance, marketing and small business development. Nevin has earned certifications in Internet marketing and economic development and has taught computers and business at the college and university level, as well as starting and operating multiple businesses over his career.

Nevin is the founder of StartUP Sault Ste. Marie - part of Startup Canada, and the author of many articles and two books on small business - including the Amazon.com best-selling 25 Money-Making Businesses You Can Start in Your Spare Time.

In his spare time he enjoys spending time with family, writing about business and technology, and exploring online business models and other opportunities.

Visit Nevin's website: www.nevinbuconjic.com

Follow on Facebook at: www.facebook.com/NevinBuconjic
Follow on Twitter: @nevinbuconjic
Visit Nevin's Amazon.com Author Page

Other books by Nevin Buconjic

25 Money-Making Businesses You Can Start in Your Spare Time

ENDNOTES

1 http://en.wikipedia.org/wiki/Richard_Branson

2 https://www.wsj.com/articles/SB10001424052970204542404577157113178985408

3 The $100 Startup: Reinvent the Way You Make A Living, Do What You Love, and Create a New Future, Chris Guillebeau, 2012.

4 http://www.entrepreneur.com/encyclopedia/term/82436.html

5 http://www.entrepreneurship.org/en/resource-center/assessing-industry-potential.aspx

6 https://www.inc.com/sean-wise/7-things-i-learned-in-business-school-that-arent-true-in-2018.html

7 The $100 Startup: Reinvent the Way You Make A Living, Do What You Love, and Create a New Future, Chris Guillebeau, 2012.

8 http://www.ontcfdc.com/frame1.asp

9 http://www.startupnation.com/business-articles/1164/1/AT_Small-Business-Capital.asp

10 http://ca.finance.yahoo.com/news/kickstarters-10-biggest-success-stories-180917980.html

11 https://www.polygon.com/2018/5/31/17412946/atari-console-pre-order-crowdfunding-campaign-successful

12 http://bottomline.nbcnews.com/_news/2012/08/08/13181500-ex-google-exec-helps-students-avoid-corporate-life?lite

[13] https://www.canada.ca/en/revenue-agency/services/tax/businesses/topics/gst-hst-businesses/charge-gst/charge-gst-hst.html

[14] https://www.sba.gov/business-guide/launch-your-business/get-federal-and-state-tax-id-numbers

[15] https://www.digitalcommerce360.com/article/us-ecommerce-sales/

[16] http://globelink.ca/wp-content/uploads/2016/01/Globe-Newspaper-MediaKit-2017-Q2-a.pdf

[17] http://www.adweek.com/news/advertising-branding/groupm-global-web-ad-spend-16-percent-2011-139483

[18] 2018 Social Media Marketing Industry Report, Michael Stelzner, Social Media Examiner, 2018

www.ingramcontent.com/pod-product-compliance
Lightning Source LLC
Chambersburg PA
CBHW031415210526
45464CB00005B/1894